Contents

The Romance Writers' Phrase Book

Jean Kent & Candace Shelton

A Perigee Book

A Perigee Book
Published by The Berkley Publishing Group
A member of Penguin Putnam Inc.
375 Hudson Street
New York, New York 10014

Published simultaneously in Canada by
General Publishing Co. Limited, Toronto.

The Penguin Putnam Inc. World Wide Web site address is
http://www.penguinputnam.com

Designed by Richard Oriolo

Library of Congress Cataloging-in-Publication Data

Kent, Jean Salter.
The romance writers' phrase book.
"A Perigee book."
1. Love stories—Authorship. 2. English language—
Terms and phrases. I. Shelton, Candace. II. Title.
PN3377.5.L68K46 1984 808.3 83-22947
ISBN 0-399-51002-8

First Perigeen edition: 1984

Printed in the United States of America
19 20 21 22 23 24 25 26 27 28

Introduction

This book is written for romance writers who, like myself, have worked like an ox to get that perfect manuscript out to a publisher only to have it returned posthaste with a terse rejection slip. Occasionally, some thoughtful editor would add a note at the bottom of the printed form, but it always said the same thing: "Nice story, but it lacks romantic tension."

"What do you mean?" I'd argue. "I had tension in my book and excitement and interesting characters, everything it takes to make the best-seller list. Why didn't you buy it?"

I belong to a writers' group that meets every week to critique each other's manuscripts. Through the group I found an agent who was willing to take a look at one of my romance novels. I sent my best shot, of course, only to have it come back in the return mail. With it was a very polite letter from the editor telling me that the book had a nice story but lacked romantic tension. So what else is new? But the editor was kind enough to add one more line—a vital one: *You need more tags!*

Tags? What are they? Anyone ever hear of one?

Yes. My agent for one, and everyone else in the publishing business for another.

Patiently, my agent explained that tags are those little descriptive phrases that spell the difference between success and failure. They are short one-liners that are so skillfully tucked into the dialogue and laced through the narrative that the reader isn't even aware of them. But they're there. The reader might not see them, but you can be sure she *feels* them. These tags are the life's breath of the romance novel. They're the difference between a cold, factual report and an eager, pulsing, sensuous story that whisks the reader out of this world into a rapturous dream of wondrous love.

Vaguely, I was beginning to get the idea, but because I'm a little dense sometimes I asked, "Could you give me an example?"

My agent was kind enough to oblige. Here's the example:

Old way: He reached out and touched her arm.

New way: A tingling of excitement raced through her as his fingers trailed sensuously down her arm.

WOW! What a difference!

"But that's just one description," I complained. "Couldn't you give me about a thousand more?"

"Sorry, but you'll have to do that yourself."

So we did.

Another woman in my writers' group, Candy Shelton, was having the same trouble, so we decided that we were going to take some time off from our novels and concentrate on writing tags. We read for months.

Gradually, very gradually, I might add, the tempo of the romance novel began to seep into our weary brains. Eventually, our perseverance started to pay off and descriptive phrases began popping up everywhere. The only trouble was, we'd keep forgetting them, so we got notebooks and proceeded to jot everything down. Pretty soon, the notebooks were full, but they were so jumbled up that they were useless. We realized that if we were going to put these tags to work for us, we'd have to categorize them somehow.

We spent days trying to decide how to do this and weeks getting all the tags into the right categories. No wonder it took us so long. When we finally pulled the whole thing together, we were amazed to discover that we had over three thousand tags!

They're all here between the covers of this book, but I hope you don't treat this list as the easy way out. These tags were not designed to be copied into your manuscript verbatim, but are here to help you create your own tags, to stimulate your imagination, get the mind in gear. Eventually, you'll begin to feel the mood and tone of the scenes, understand the joys and sorrows and hopes of your heroine, sense the pulsing rhythm of your compelling hero. And when you can do this, you're on your way.

This is your workbook. Use it. Make notes in it. Mark it up. Add to it. Rearrange it. Cross out things you don't like. The point is, put this book to work for you, and you'll find it's the most valuable tool you have.

Even now, with several romances under my belt, I find myself referring to *The Romance Writers' Phrase Book* when I'm struggling with a new story. After browsing through a few pages, my mind unconsciously drifts into the tempo of the romance novel and soon the words begin to flow as smoothly as the sensuous movement of a passionate love scene.

Jean Salter Kent

Physical Characteristics—Female

Body

her hose felt like sheaths of clammy cloth on her exceptionally pretty legs

her slender white neck

her figure was curving and regal

her hips tapered into long straight legs

her soft ivory shoulders beckoned to him

she was tall and graceful

her wrists were delicate

her fingers were strong and slim

she had a slim, wild beauty

her jutting breasts and narrow waist

she was slender, reedlike, willowy

she had fine hips and shapely thighs

her features were dainty, her wrists small

her throat looked warm and shapely above a low-cut bodice

a belt around her waist defined its smallness

the apricot and milky color of her skin

the suggestion of nubile curves beneath her dress

her body was slender, her hips slim

the lace at her throat parted and he saw the hollow of her neck filled with soft shadows

her skin was like peach-tinted cream

moist satin of her breasts

the melting softness of her body

the black velvet of her dress heightened the translucence of her face and neck

she was petite and flowerlike

she was slender, dark, and fiery with eyes that glowed and pierced

with long sensitive fingers

her seductive young body and wholesome good looks

her uptilted breasts and curved hips

her smooth bosom and arms

she stood up slowly, her body tall and trim

firm high-perched breasts

a slim waist which flared into agilely rounded hips

long, lithe thighs

Face

her facial bones were delicately carved, her mouth full
her face was austere, her manner haughty
she had a genial mouth and sparkling eyes
her face was pink with eagerness
her heightened color subsided
her high, exotic cheekbones in a delicate face
her face was a perfect oval
her face was arresting, irregular
she had a square chin and a wide mouth
her temptingly curved mouth
her face was well modeled and feminine
her smooth skin glowed with pale gold undertones
her nose exquisitely dainty
she had a chin of iron determination
her ivory face had a musk-rose flush on the cheekbones
her faintly rosy mouth
her complexion was white and illusive pink
the dusty rose of her cheeks
her lips full and rounded over even teeth
her patrician features
generously curved parted lips
her pretty Grecian nose
her lashes swept down across her cheekbones

her face white beneath her tan

a quiet oval face, dark, and rather delicate

the living moistness of her full red mouth

her nose was straight, short and charming

the wind whipped color into her cheeks

there was a soft color in her sweet curled lips

there was both delicacy and strength in her face

her soft cheeks were of rose and pearl

the flush on her pale cheek was like the flush of sunset on snow

her oval face was daintily pointed

her mouth was a smiling rosy flower

the corners of her mouth turned upwards more than they turned down

her face was pale, but proud

Hair

---

her hair was a rich, glowing auburn

her thick dark hair hung in long graceful curves over her shoulders

she had a wealth of dark hair

her head was capped by a mass of bronze-gold hair

loose tendrils of hair softened her face

her long golden hair was like strands of lustrous glass

her hair tumbled carelessly down her back

copper ringlets curled on her forehead and on her nape

her hair blew about her

an escaping curl fell over her forehead

her fair hair blown into disarray by the wind

her hair was the pale yellow of a field of grain

her ash-blonde hair clustered in short curls around a heart-shaped face

wisps of hair framed her face

dark hair swinging about her proud shoulders

her hair was a honey colored, curly cap

her hair was a luminous buttercup yellow

the golden mist of her hair

her light brown curls were wind blown

her hair was a cobweb of silvery gold

her hair was black, like shining glass

her dark hair glistened like polished wood

small curls twisted and crinkled across her forehead

tiny curling tendrils escaped the heavy silken mass of black hair

the jet-black hair flowed from a center part

her hair was disheveled, a black aura encircling her head

wind gently fluffed her soft dark hair

her red-gold hair, blue eyes, and fair skin

her hair was the black of a starless night

her bright auburn hair gleamed with shadows of deep gold or rich red wispy bangs fell across her forehead

the wind kicked at her curls

Other

---

she was gentle, serenely wise, and beautiful

she had a look of loving to pamper herself

she looked more delicate and ethereal than ever

a strength that did not lessen her femininity

she moved like a model or a dancer

her gentle and overwhelming beauty

she paused, broadcasting a regal certainty

her beauty was exquisite, fragile

she looked ethereal, unreal in the dim light

she had developed a strength and stamina at odds with the slenderness of her body

she was volatile by nature

she could be as playful as a girl or as composed as an intelligent woman

the animation of her character was enchanting

she carried herself confidently, aware of the appreciative glances

Physical Characteristics—Male

Body

his hand was rough and gave her a sense of protection

his tall, black-clad figure stiffened

he was tall, rawboned, beardless, with an ingenuously appealing face

his massive shoulders filled the coat he wore

his stance emphasized the force of his thighs and the slimness of his hips

he looked tough, lean, and sinewy

the muscles rippling under his white shirt quickened her pulse

she wondered if his broad shoulders ever tired of the burden he carried

the very way he stood there told you he had made it

he stood tall and straight like a towering spruce

a tall, ascetic-looking man

his arm was bare and silky with hairs

his powerful well-muscled body moved with easy grace

a handsome compact man who walked with a spring in his step

he stood as if he prided himself on his good looks

his hands, beautiful, long-fingered, and strong

small-boned of medium height

his shoulders, a yard wide and molded bronze

he walked with nonchalant grace

he towered over the other men by a full eight inches

his movements were swift, full of grace and virility

he was slender rather than tall

his long, sturdy Viking legs

his muscular arms were bare

she looked up at the powerful set of shoulders

he carried himself with a commanding air of self-confidence

he stood there, devilishly handsome

he looked very powerful, his chest broad and muscular

she took in his tempting, attractive male physique

her eyes froze on his long, lean form

the dark figure of a man, big and powerful

as his broad shoulders disappeared around the corner

tall, handsome, with a beautifully proportioned body

she was acutely conscious of his tall, athletic physique

the rich outlines of his shoulders strained against the fabric his legs, brown and firm as tree trunks

his open shirt revealed a muscular chest covered with crisp brown hair

his hands were big and square

he had a wide-shouldered, rangy body

his long, sinewy legs

Face

---

there was an inherent strength in his face

his ruggedly handsome face was vaguely familiar

his compelling blue eyes, the firm features, the confident set of his shoulders

the shadow of his beard gave him an even more manly aura

his profile spoke of power and ageless strength

his firm mouth curled as if always on the edge of laughter

his face was bronzed by wind and sun

his lips were firm and sensual

the set of his chin suggested a stubborn streak

his jaw thrust forward

his square jaw tensed visibly

his fat face melted into a buttery smile

dark eyes framing a handsome square face

his bulbous nose dominated his meaty features

his profile was sharp and confident

the clear-cut lines of his profile

his profile, dark against the moonlight

he had a generous mouth, an aquiline nose

his classically handsome features

his lips parted in a dazzling display of straight, white teeth

his smile was wide, his teeth strikingly white in his tanned face

his smooth olive skin stretched over high cheekbones

he had a pale gold, sensitive face

he was handsome with dark eyes and a secret expression

his handsome face was kindled with a sort of passionate beauty

he held his head high with pride

his profile was strong and rigid

reflected light glimmered over his handsome face like beams of icy radiance

his teeth, even and white, contrasted pleasingly with his olive skin

his skin pulled taut over the elegant ridge of his cheekbones

his brows and eyes were startling against his fair skin and light hair

his aquiline nose, straight forehead

he had a humorous, kindly mouth

his fair skin magnified the inky blackness of his eyes

there were touches of humor around the mouth and near the eyes

drops of moisture clung to his damp forehead

a new contentment on his face

his mouth was thin with a cynical twist to it

his strong features held a certain sensuality

his boldly handsome face smiled warmly down at her

a muscle clenched along his jaw

the pain was carved in merciless lines on his face

there were age lines about his mouth and eyes, muting his youth with strength

his handsome face was reserved

his profile was rugged and somber

he had a stubborn, arrogant face

pleasure softened his granitelike face

his features were so perfect, so symmetrical, that any more delicacy would have made him too beautiful for a man

Hair

his black hair gleamed in the lights

his thick hair tapering neatly to his collar

a wan shaft of sun struck his hair and it gleamed like dark gold

manly wisps of dark hair curled against the V of his open shirt

he had thick tawny-gold hair

a swath of wavy hair fell casually on his forehead

preoccupied with his blonde hair and long slim legs

his dark curling hair was cut short

his hair was black and silky straight

his hair was the color of field oats

his full black hair flowed from his face like a crest

with a thick crop of yellow hair

his light brown hair had sandy-red highlights

dank tendrils of hair curling on his forehead

his hair ruffled by the breeze

one lock fell a little forward onto his head

he was tall with black, unruly hair

the fine curly golden hair on his arms

his dark hair, just graying at the temples, was still full

long sideburns flecked with gray

his light hair was a stark contrast to his deep tan

Other

---

his well-groomed appearance was incongruous with his suntanned skin

he was a massive, self-confident presence

he had an air of authority and the appearance of one who demanded instant obedience

even in a crowd, his presence was compelling

there was an air of isolation about his tall figure

the clean, light look of him impressed her

his cold urbanity was only slightly disturbed

he had a commanding manner

there was a restless energy about his movements

he was devastatingly handsome

she felt the power that coiled within him as he walked

his arresting good looks totally captured her attention

his nature as full of sunshine as his looks

he was attractive and unscrupulous enough to take any woman

he had a ruggedness and vital power that attracted her

his dress was simple but rich

women found him deliciously appealing

a tall, dark figure stepped from the shadows

there was a firm strength in him

he had acquired a polished veneer

he had a monopoly on virility

his attitude of self-command and studied relaxation

he had the craggy look of unfinished sculpture

the heat emanating from his body

nearly colliding with his powerful body

the tantalizing smell of his after-shave

he exuded masculinity

an air of command exuded from him

he was even more stunningly virile than ever

he had an innately captivating presence

Body Movements

Fingers

lightly he fingered a loose tendril of hair on her cheek

lifting one hand, he slipped his fingers under the shoulder strap

she was careful not to let her fingers touch his

his fingers took her arm with gentle authority

his fingers biting deeply into her shoulder

his fingers stroked her arm sensuously

his fingers clamped over her trembling chin

his fingers wrapped around the dark fabric of her sleeve

his fingers slid sensuously over her bare arm

touching her trembling lips with one finger

his fingers pressing into her back

his fingers trailed down her temple

she reached out, lacing his fingers with her own

his fingers were cool and smooth as they touched hers

mockingly coy, she ran her finger along her jaw

his finger tenderly traced the line of her cheekbone and jaw

her fingers drummed distractedly on her crossed knee

his fingers, tapered and strong, caressed the mug

his fingers brushed her collarbone, lingering there too long to be an accident

the muscles were hard beneath her fingertips

placing long, calloused fingers on the desk before him

his fingers curved under her chin

she thrust her fingers through his thick hair

her arm trapped in his iron fingers

his fingers dug into her soft flesh

her fingers fluttered to her neck

his fingers were warm and strong as he grasped hers

he brushed aside her trembling fingers

she touched his cheeks, the skin cold beneath her fingertips

his muscles tensed suddenly under her fingertips

as soon as her reaching fingers touched the warmth of his outreached hand, she felt safe

the soft brushing of his fingers against her cheek

leaning down, she slowly curled her fingers in his hair

his fingers touched hers and she had the wildest urge to jump back

Hands and Arms

he put his hand on her shoulder in a possessive gesture
she reached out and clutched at his hand
he wound a hand in her hair
he held up a hand to silence her
she withdrew her hand quickly and turned away
putting his hands up to push the wet hair off his face
hastily she drew her hand away
his free hand moved recklessly to her neck
she placed her hand on his forearm
his hands trembled with eagerness
she was halted by an iron grip on her wrist
his arm firmly around her waist
a change in the pressure of his hands on her shoulders
his hand came down over hers possessively
stretching his arm across the back of her seat
the warmth of personal contact in his hand
folding her hands in a pose of tranquillity
her slender hands unconsciously twisted together
restlessly, her hand stroked the arm of the chair
she felt his hand brush the hair from her neck
covering her hands with his own
she lifted her arms to cover her breasts
slamming a hand on the desk in front of him

he reached out and caught her hand in his

his hand remained on her shoulder for a moment too long

a protective hand pressed her closer to him

she turned away, her hands clenched stiffly at her sides

he halted her escape with a firm hand on her arm

he touched her elbow lightly, urging yet protective

reaching for the solid strength of his arm

his hands resting on his hips

stroking his chin, he regarded her carefully

throwing up his hands, he sighed

he grasped the neck of the heavy muslin nightgown

he placed a restraining hand on her arm

then his hands relaxed, resting lightly on her

he pulled his hand free of hers

he smoothed her hair

lightly taking her hand

she closed her hand over his

she smoothed his hair with her hand and loved him with her eyes

he held out his hands, offering an apology

cupping her chin, he searched her upturned face

she flattened her palms against her dress

she pushed back a wayward strand of dark hair

he put his hand under her chin, turning her toward him

in a defensive gesture, she folded her arms across her chest

he cupped her chin tenderly in his warm hand

she stretched out her arms to touch him

his hand slid down her arm and tightened around her wrist

he clutched her hand with both of his

he made a dismissing gesture

he took hold of her hand and pulled her back

she felt her fists bunching at her sides

he waved his hand in a gesture of dismissal

putting his arm around her waist, he squeezed her affectionately

she paused, looked at his hand, then shook it

nervously she ran her hands through her hair

he stopped her with a raised hand

she flicked an imaginary speck of dirt from her dress

his strong hands circled her waist and lifted her down

she flung her hands out in despair

his flesh met hers in a warm clasp

his hand lingered a moment too long in its hold

she raised her hand to shelter her eyes

he drove his fist into the palm of his hand

he rubbed the back of his hand across his mouth

he made a slight gesture with his right hand

his arms spread expansively

he was massaging her arm in a circular motion

the hand, massive and strong, spun her around

he touched her cheek in a wistful gesture

he caressed her cheek, smiling sadly

without warning a hand closed over her right shoulder

she made no effort to retrieve her hand

caressing her cheek with the knuckle of his forehand

he pushed stray tendrils of hair away from her cheek

she wiped her cheeks with the back of her hand

his hand was strong, firm, protective

her hand moved of its own volition from his cheek to his jawline

she threw up her hands in disgust

he folded his hands together in a comfortable gesture

pushing the reddish-gold curls back from her ears

she threw her hands over her face

clenching and unclenching her right hand

he slammed one fist against the other

gestured in a sweeping motion with one arm

he cupped the glass in his hand

his hands tightened on her arm

he dusted off his hands

she promptly disengaged her hands

his hands locked together behind his back

she clapped a hand to her cheek

her hands buried in the thickness of his hair

she smoothed her brow with both hands

she straightened to relieve the ache in her shoulders

with a few swift strokes he closed the circle

Head Motions, Nods

---

she answered, turning her face away from him

she bent her head and studied her hands

she tilted her head in a nod and left the room

he shook his head decisively

she inclined her head in compliance

she gave a forced smile and a tense nod of consent

he shook his head as if genuinely concerned

she gave him a curt nod of farewell

he inclined his blond head

he nodded perfunctorily and turned back

he answered with an impersonal nod

she shook her head in dismay

he nodded gloomily

he nodded, not trusting himself to speak

she wagged her head

she shook her head violently

she nodded back at him without speaking

she leaned her head back and gazed into his eyes

jauntily he cocked his blond head to one side

he nodded complacently

with an adventurous toss of her head

lifting her head, straining back against his arm

she cradled her head in her trembling hands

his head swung lazily to the other side

raising her chin, she assumed all the dignity she could muster

dipping his head slightly, he said

he bent his head slightly forward

he nodded dubiously

she inspected it quickly, then looked up suspiciously

he lifted his head alertly

she shook her head disapprovingly

he smiled and inclined his head

with a tip of his head, he motioned her to the chair beside him

a casual polite nod from an uninterested stranger

she inclined her head in a small gesture of thanks

he inclined his head in a deep gesture

tilting her head back, she peered at his face

he nodded with a taut jerk of his head

he bowed his head and murmured

she stiffened and haughtily tossed her head

then inclined his sleek head

she leaned lightly into him, tilting her face toward his

he indicated by a motion of his head that he would listen

she tossed her head again

he nodded and chuckled at her

she tipped her face to the sun

he gave her a grudging nod

he looked briefly over his shoulder

she nodded woodenly

tilting her head, she saw him

he shook his head in utter disbelief

he gave her a brief nod and walked briskly away

tilting her head to one side, she stole a slanted look at him

she wrinkled her nose and shook her head

he swung his head around to look up at her

she tossed her head and gave an irritable tug at her sleeve

her head bowed and she remained in an attitude of frozen stillness

she tilted her chin up, wiped her eyes, and turned away

she shook her head negatively

she raised her chin with a cool stare in his direction

Sitting, Standing

she fell into a chair and laid her head on the desk

snatching her wrist away, she stood up

he dropped down beside her, facing her

she pushed herself to a standing position

standing, she straightened her shoulders and cleared her throat

she leaned back in her chair, relaxing and soaking up the sun

he sat beside her and stroked the damp curls from her face

with his powerful hands, he yanked her to her feet

there was no time to stand and stare

he reached out and hauled her from the chair

nearly collapsing into the chair as her knees buckled

she watched him as he rose to his feet

he stood up and pushed his hands deep into his pockets

he stood over her, his hands on his hips

he stood there, boldly intimidating

they sat silently for a long time

she rose fluidly from the chair

she slid gracefully into the wicker-backed chair

she jerked to her feet

he rose in one fluid motion

she flopped onto the bed with a grateful sigh

she settled into the deep red cushions

she rose from her seat as if propelled by an explosive force

as she had a chance to sit back, she became aware of another kind of excitement

she stood frozen in the doorway

she stood motionless in the middle of the room

he raised himself up on one elbow

he sat forward and looked at her intently

he wedged himself into the seat next to her

he sat very still, his eyes narrow

she awoke with a start and jolted upright

she stood and watched, silently waiting to see

Turns, Shrugs, Leaning

---

he gave an impatient shrug

he spun and was gone

she drew back into the room and leaned against the wall

she swiveled quickly, turning her back

roughly he thrust her away from him

she turned with a start when someone touched her arm

he lounged casually against the door frame

he shrugged matter-of-factly

he leaned toward her, his eyes cold

he leaned back on his elbows

he shrugged dismissively

he shrugged his shoulders in mock resignation

he swung her around, revealing her slender legs and thighs

she managed to shrug and say, offhandedly

she leaned back and closed her eyes

he leaned back, sizing her up

leaning forward in his chair, in a controlled voice he said

she turned away, not waiting for an answer

their bodies began to sway to and fro

leaning her elbow on the table, she rested her chin in her hand

leaning against the door for a moment, she tried to gather strength

with a deliberately casual movement, she turned and faced him

he moved his shoulders in a shrug of anger

turning blindly, she stumbled

she swiveled slowly, her delight growing

he leaned back, sipping the liquid contentedly

he hunched over, his arms resting on his thighs

suddenly she found herself being spun around

she leaned against the taut smoothness of his shoulder

he leaned back and fit his fingers together

she leaned toward him, exhaling with agitation

she leaned back, suppressing a sigh

he spread his hands regretfully and shrugged

she leaned lightly into him, tilting her face toward his

he stopped in midstride and turned

she stopped suddenly and slowly turned in a circle

Body in Motion

---

the tall figure turned and headed toward her

her steps slowed as she pondered

looking up as she approached, he quite openly studied her

she strolled about, nodding at a few people as she moved

she moved away, her jaw tightening

he looked at her intently, then strode to the door

she had to step away from his tense, hard body

she shifted indignantly from foot to foot

taking a deep, unsteady breath, she stepped back

she was abruptly caught by the elbow and firmly escorted

he pulled her along behind him

they both turned and walked on silently

he disappeared quickly into the crowd

his footsteps thundering down the hall

smothering a groan, she stepped back

he came close, looking down at her intensely

by tacit consent, they both turned and walked away

he worked off his excess energy by pacing

he stopped and inhaled a deep breath

she took an abrupt step toward him

walking slowly, her hips swaying

she walked with stiff dignity

he walked forward, stopping in front of her

he turned on his heel and strode to the door

with a springy bounce, she was gone

she hurried, not stopping to explain

she withdrew from his arms and moved to the right

reluctantly, he walked, his movements stiff and awkward

she walked grandly to the chaise lounge and arranged herself over its curving surface

he paced the room for the remaining time

she stepped out of his encircling arms

she moved closer to him, her head thrust forward

he strolled forward and extended a hand

his lithe body moving beside her

she moved easily but impatiently

she asked faintly, drawing a step nearer to him

with long, purposeful strides

each stride was fluid

Other

---

she hugged her knees to her

she froze, mind and body benumbed

he stretched his long legs casually before him

she yanked away from him

an electrifying shudder reverberated through her

her mind and body were finally moving together

she remained absolutely motionless for a moment

licking her lips nervously

she could feel the supple muscles tense

she felt, rather than saw, his shocked movement

somehow she managed to face him

in a lightning-fast motion

she hugged her arms to her
he dragged her back hard against him
visibly trembling with intensity
scrupulously, she buttoned her dress
she scuffed the toe of her shoe in the sand
she replaced the receiver with a whoop
he pulled reluctantly away and held her at arms' length
he pulled her close to his side and they walked together
he shuffled through the papers impatiently
he moved closer until he left her no room at all
she swallowed hard and squared her shoulders
his gentle nudge brought her back from her daydreams
he moved in an instinctive gesture of comfort
he slapped her heartily on the back
she drew an invisible pattern on the tablecloth
he touched his forehead slightly in a mock salute
his thigh barely touched hers
he heard her and then froze into blankness
she drew her legs up, placing her feet on the chair seat
sliding down in the water until she was submerged to her chin
he reached out, swinging her around to face him
she stood frozen in the doorway
she stood motionless in the middle of the room
leisurely he stretched his long legs
then she rocked back gracefully on her heels

contentedly she rested against the warm lines of his body

he grinned and straightened his shoulders

he wheeled back to her

she watched his broad back

he straightened, sighing loudly

he stiffened at the question

she looked up to see him pause just inside the door

he picked her up and swung her around excitedly

she stopped, her mind frozen

he raised himself up on one elbow

roughly, he thrust her away from him

Facial Expressions

Brows

his brows drew together in an agonized expression
he tilted his brow, looking at her uncertainly
the dark eyebrows arched mischievously
his brow pulled into an affronted frown
his brows drew together in an angry frown
his eyebrows raised inquiringly
his brows flickered a little
raising fine, arched eyebrows, she protested
his left eyebrow rose a fraction
his eyebrows shot up in surprise
her eyebrows rose in amazement
he said with a significant lifting of his brows
the dark eyebrows slanted in a frown
unconsciously her brow furrowed
his brows set in a straight line

an eyebrow raised in amused contempt

her brow creased with worry

his brow wrinkled with his contemptuous thoughts

the lines of concentration deepened along his brows and under his eyes

he quirked his eyebrow questioningly

his brows drew downward in a frown

an arched eyebrow indicated his humorous surprise

her brow was high and rounded

Mouth and Jaw

she noted his set face, his clamped mouth and fixed eyes

a muscle flicked angrily at his jaw

her mouth tightened when she looked up to see a familiar face

the tensing of her jaw betrayed her deep frustrations

a muscle quivered at his jaw

nervously she moistened her dry lips

there was a suspicious line at the corners of his mouth

staring blankly with her mouth open

she pressed her lips together in anger

she bit her lip to stifle a grin

her lips parted in surprise

his jaw clenched, his eyes slightly narrowed

his mouth thinning with displeasure

his mouth was tight and grim
the line of his mouth tightened a fraction more
her mouth lifting in mute invitation
she clamped her jaw tight and stared
a circle of ice ringing her mouth
his mouth twisted wryly
she managed to reply through stiff lips
his mouth twisted into a threat
she set her chin in a stubborn line
a tremor touched her smooth, marblelike lips
he drew his lips in thoughtfully

Smiles

the smile in his eyes contained a sensuous flame
an irresistibly devastating grin
the warmth of his smile echoed in his voice
his infectious grin set the tone
she met the smile and the hand which was offered
the beginning of a smile tipped the corners of his mouth
resting her chin on her hand, a bemused smile on her lips
his mouth curved into an unconscious smile
his smile widened in approval
her smile faded a little when he looked at her
she smiled to herself as he spoke

a thoughtful smile curved her mouth

he smiled with beautiful candor

an easy smile played at the corners of his mouth

she was unaware of the captivating picture she made when she smiled

his smile was courteous as he left them

before his appealing smile, her defenses melted away

she broke into an open, friendly smile

a smile found its way through the mask of uncertainty

she found it impossible not to return his disarming smile

he offered her a forgiving smile

he grinned back briefly with no trace of his former animosity

he gave her a smile that sent her pulses racing

a smile remained on his extremely handsome face

he stood up, smiling with satisfaction

she smiled but didn't answer

his smile had a spark of eroticism

he turned, easing into a smile

she smiled in contentment, smelling the faint citrus scent of his after-shave

he exchanged a smile with her, then shook his head

then a grin overtook his features

his smile relaxed measurably

she smiled tentatively

a small smile of enchantment touched her lips

they looked at each other and smiled in earnest

successfully disarming her with his smile
his smile matched hers in liveliness
they shared a smile
his face split into a wide grin
he rewarded her with a larger smile of his own
his grin flashed briefly, dazzling against his olive skin
he smiled, thinking about it
a smile ruffled his mouth
one corner of his mouth was pulled into a slight smile
the glow of his smile warmed her across the room
his smile was without malice, almost apologetic
he smiled easily
with a slow, secret smile, she understood
a smile trembled over her lips
his smile was as intimate as a kiss
she broke into a wide, open smile
his smile brought an immediate softening to his features
her face creased into a sudden smile
she managed a small, tentative smile
he walked up to her with a grin of amusement
in a desperate attempt to resist the captivating smile
his whole face spread into a smile
her smile was eager and alive with affection and delight
the even whiteness of her smile was dazzling
he offered her a sudden, arresting smile
his grin was irresistibly devastating

the magnetism of his smile

she offered him a small, shy smile

her mouth curved into an unconscious smile

his tight expression relaxed into a smile

the warmth of his laugh sent shivers down her spine

drawing in a slow, steady smile of happiness

he smiled his mercurial smile

his smile was boyishly affectionate

she smiled with an air of pleasure

she smiled comfortably to herself

two dimples appeared as if loving fingers had squeezed her cheek

she was smiling and radiant

his mouth curved with tenderness

the smile turned to a chuckle

a depth to her smile that had been missing too long

she looked up, flashing a smile of thanks

he smiled suggestively

a secretive smile softened her lips

he broke into a leisurely smile

a soft and loving curve touched her lips

he smiled at her as if she were a small child

lately, she had cultivated a certain smile

she grinned mischievously

Negative Expressions

---

his mouth spread into a thin-lipped smile

his mouth pulled into a sour grin

his lips twisted into a cynical smile

offering her a distracted nod, he returned her smile

her faint smile held a touch of sadness

she stopped suddenly and smiled in exasperation

it was a bleak, tight-lipped smile

crestfallen, her smile quickly faded

she smiled smoothly, betraying nothing of her annoyance

they exchanged a polite, simultaneous smile

there was a thin smile on his lips as he

a satanic smile spread across his thin lips

his smile was without humor

she was unable to face his mocking smile

he contradicted her with a smile that set her teeth on edge

she managed a tremulous smile

he shot her a twisted smile

he smiled blandly

his mouth took on an unpleasant twist

he gazed at her with a bland half smile

she realized with a wry smile

his smile did not indicate compliance

a half smile crossed his face

she pasted on a smile of nonchalance

frowning into the glass

his distinguished face had become brooding

his face became a marble effigy of contempt

a warning cloud settled on his features

a cold, congested expression settled on his face

she was silenced by his dark, angry expression

his implacable expression was unnerving

his expression was a mask of stone

suddenly his face went grim

he was a glum-faced man

there was an arrested expression on his face

he frowned with cold fury

he frowned, his eyes level under drawn brows

she saw the frown set into his features

his mouth dipped into an even deeper frown

a stern-faced expression

his expression was taut and derisive

his expression was one of pained tolerance

his expression grew hard and resentful

his face was marked with loathing

cold dignity created a stony mask of his face

a watchful fixity in his face

his dark face set in a vicious expression

the familiar mask descended once again

his expression held a note of mockery

he had a hard, cold-eyed smile

still smiling, his rapier glance passed over her

one corner of his mouth twisted upward

he smiled benignly, as if dealing with a temperamental child

she took a deep breath and adjusted her smile

his brittle smile softened slightly

she forced a demure smile

his derisive grin was not to be tolerated

his smile vanished, wiped away by astonishment

his expression was tight with strain

he then frowned in exasperation

a melancholy frown flitted across his features

she looked away swiftly at the sight of his scowl

Other

---

his expression stilled and grew serious

she watched his expression of hate change to desire

he said smoothly, with no expression on his face

his expressive face changed and became almost somber

he looked at her enigmatically

an intense but secret expression

her face brightened at the suggestion

she felt her flesh color

once more, his face displayed an uncanny awareness

a look of implacable determination on his face

his face brightened at the sight of her

his look was one of faint amusement

she kept her features deceptively composed

he missed the questioning gaze that passed between them

though he didn't answer, his face spoke for him

she was keenly aware of his scrutiny

for an instant a wistfulness stole into his expression

his expression was that of complete unconcern

his face was smiling, but work-hardened

across her pale and beautiful face a dim flush raced like a fever

his countenance was immobile

the look on his face mingled eagerness and tenderness

there was an almost imperceptible note of pleading in his face

she flushed, but remained silent

this time she kept her expression under stern restraint

an inexplicable look of withdrawal came over his face

his aloofness showed in his face

she eyed him with a calculating expression

he weighed her with a critical squint

a momentary look of discomfort crossed her face

his expression was hungry and lustful

Humor

Amusement

her reaction seemed to amuse him

he put the matter aside with sudden good humor

there was something warm and enchanting in his humor

she enjoyed the gentle sparring as much as he did

her companion regarded her with amusement

his eyes grew openly amused

she loved his gentle camaraderie, his subtle wit

he spoke in jesting quips

she looked at him with amused wonder

amusement flickered in the eyes that met hers

seeing the amusement in his eyes, she laughed

a flash of humor crossed her face

the glint of humor finally returning

friendly, smiling, bantering in a relaxed manner

her perpetual merriment

his mouth quirked with humor

for some reason, he found her displeasure amusing

amused but unmoved by her quick retort

he turned up his smile a notch

there was a pale blue lightning of amusement between his lashes

he spoke in his casual, jesting way

he was casually amused

he was teasing her, affectionately, not maliciously

grimaced in good humor

her amusement swiftly died

he felt a ripple of mirth

his mouth twitched with amusement

her lips trembled with the need to smile

Laughter

---

he threw back his head and let out a great peal of laughter

she brought her hand up to stifle her giggles

her gentle laugh rippled through the air

she laughed infectiously

he chuckled with happy memory

she laughed in sheer joy

she tried to suppress a giggle

when he laughed he seemed ten years younger

she murmured, half laughing half crying

her sense of humor took over and she laughed in answer

she couldn't control her burst of laughter

she was laughing gently

she laughed and there was a little hysteria in her voice

he laughed as if sincerely amused

there was a trace of laughter in her voice

he laughed richly

his laugh was triumphant

her undiluted laughter

his laughter floated up from his throat

his laugh was marvelous, catching

his laugh was deep, warm, and rich

he chuckled with a dry and cynical sound

a deep chuckle greeted her

she couldn't help laughing aloud to herself

he laughed hoarsely and bitterly

in spite of herself, she chuckled

her laughter had a sharp edge

his laugh was scornful

her cold resentment vanished as she couldn't keep herself from laughing

he stared at her and then burst out laughing

his laughter was a full-hearted sound

the teasing laughter was back in his eyes

his laugh was low, throaty

he laughed in a deep, jovial way
she managed a choking laugh
his laugh broke off, his eyes smoldered
his smile deepened into laughter
she was barely able to keep the laughter from her voice
he threw his head back and roared with laughter
she couldn't help herself as she burst out laughing
rocked with the laughter of revelers

Eyes

Expression

her wide-eyed innocence was merely a smoke screen
his eyes were cold and proud
his eyes glowed with a savage inner fire
her eyes were brilliantly intelligent
his eyes had a sheen of purpose
his eyes gleamed like glassy volcanic rock
the mystery in his eyes beckoned to her irresistibly
her eyes were full of remoteness
his eyes were sharp and assessing
his eyes were like summer lightning
his eyes were dark and insolent
her eyes were artless and serene
his eyes showed intelligence and independence of spirit
his eyes were dark and unfathomable
the eyes were compelling, magnetic

a faint light twinkled in the depths of his black eyes

her blue eyes were full of life, pain, and unquenchable warmth

her eyes had a burning, faraway look in them

his extraordinary eyes blazed and glowed

he had clear, observant eyes

his eyes were serenely compelling

dark snappy eyes looked out from his sun-toughened face

her eyes held a gleam that no makeup could improve

his eyes were flat, hard, passionless

the expression in his currant-black eyes seemed to plead for friendship

his flat, unspeaking eyes prolonged the moment

his burning eyes held her still

his pale eyes were like bits of stone

a devilish look came into his eyes

the amused look suddenly left his eyes

there was a faint glint of humor in his eyes

again, the mischievous look came into his eyes

there was a lethal calmness in his eyes

raw hurt glittered in those dark eyes

her eyes were stony with anger

hatred blazed in those eyes

his eyes were bright with merriment

a satisfied light came into his eyes

his eyes were filled with contempt

with a glint of wonder in his eyes

a strange, faintly eager look flashed in his eyes

unspoken pain was alive and glowing in his eyes

an almost hopeful glint in his eyes

his eyes were hard and filled with dislike

his eyes were full of half promises

there was a spark of some indefinable emotion in his eyes

excitement added shine to her eyes and polish to her cheeks

his eyes were icy and unresponsive

his gray eyes became flat and as unreadable as stone

her eyes glowed with enjoyment

her eyes were filled with a curious deep longing

the excited light was vivid in her eyes

his eyes brimmed with tenderness and passion

her eyes were misty and wistful

a twinkle of moonlight caught his eyes as he glanced at her

the eyes were gentle and contemplative

a gleam of interest in his gray eyes

his eyes smoldered with fire

his eyes were gentle, understanding

there was eagerness in his eyes

her eyes shone bright in the pale light of the moon

her eyes brightened with pleasure

light smoldered in his gold-flecked eyes

she couldn't dull the sparkle in her gray-green eyes

her large black eyes were filled with shifting stars

Color

dark gray-green flecked eyes

her green eyes lighted a little

the Nordic blue of his eyes

his gray eyes were like silver lightning

he had extraordinary eyes, flecked and ringed with gold

his eyes were a brilliant blue

he had depthless, jet-black eyes

his wild sapphire eyes mellowed subtly

his eyes were a tawny shade of brown

her blue eyes shone like cobalt

hard, gray eyes, like glacial ice

the olive-black eyes, unfathomable in their murky depths

eyes that were a startling blue, as blue as the summer sky

he had eyes like green ice

the shifting emerald lights of her eyes

her brilliant black button eyes were fixed on him

his eyes were even darker than sapphires

the blue of his eyes was like a cold wave

her bright, clear blue eyes were direct

her eyes were like green, polished jade

she watched with rounded blue eyes

the long lashes of her liquid brown eyes

her blue eyes flashed with azure fire

she had large green eyes under golden brows and lashes

his warm gold-green eyes were full of expectation

the firm set of his jaw, the intense brown eyes

the gold in his eyes flickered with interest

his eyes were shades of amber and green

her hazel eyes were lit from within with a golden glow

the sunlight in his blue eyes shone like bits of gleaming porcelain

she had full hazel eyes with sweeping lashes

her dark eyes were as beautiful as black satin

she had clear blue eyes ringed with black lashes

she was entranced by the chocolate of his eyes

Movement

his blue eyes met her gray ones

her eyes moved upward to his broad chest

he captured her eyes with his

his eyes came up to study her face

his eyes clung to hers, analyzing her reaction

her lids slipped down over her eyes

she raised her eyes to find him watching her

she lowered her thick, black lashes

his lids came down swiftly over his eyes

her eyes shifted from one person to the other

his eyes roamed over her figure

he winked at her broadly

he gave an exaggerated wink to her companion

his appreciative eye traveled from her sandals to her green dress

he winked when he caught her eye

her eyes darted nervously back and forth

he gave her a conspiratorial wink

her eyes grew large and liquid

eyeing him up and down covetously

his blue eyes pierced the distance between them

his eyes caught and held hers

he squinted, peering around the room

his eyes swept over her face approvingly

she looked up at him with dreamy eyes

his eyes searched her face, reaching into her thoughts

his eyes caressed her softness

his eyes probed to her very soul

her eyes sparkled as though she was playing a game

tenderly, his eyes melted into hers

his dark brown eyes softened at the sight of her

he surveyed her kindly

his blue eyes widened in accusation

his black eyes impaled her
his eyes flashed imperiously
his eyes blazed with sudden anger
his eyes flashed with outrage
his dark eyes never left hers for an instant
his eyes sparkled with the love of combat
his gray eyes bored into her
his eyes blazed down into hers
the gray eyes narrowed and hardened
she watched his eyes widen with concern
his cold brown eyes took her in
a sudden icy contempt flashed in his eyes
his eyes narrowed and his back became ramrod straight
she shot him a withering glance
she blinked, feeling lightheaded
his eyes narrowed suspiciously
her eyes widened in alarm
the blue eyes narrowed speculatively
his dark eyes flashed a gentle but firm warning
his eyes flashed in a familiar display of impatience
she dropped her eyes before his steady gaze
she watched him with a critical squint
her eyes widened with false innocence
his mercurial black eyes sharpened
he watched with a keenly observant eye
she thought she detected laughter in his eyes

a wry but indulgent glint appeared in his eyes

featherlike laugh lines crinkled around his eyes

she observed him through lowered lashes

two deep lines of worry appeared between her eyes

she observed him with her sweet musing look

suddenly his dark eyes grew wild

her eyes darted around the room in frustration

she tried to catch his eye, to communicate with him

she was able to study him freely, outwardly

he looked up lazily through half-closed lids

his gaze lowered as did his voice

his gaze returned to her again and again

he studied her face with his enigmatic gaze for an extra beat

she cast her eyes downward

she blinked, then focused her gaze

she tried not to be caught staring at him

his gaze arched slowly back and forth

he looked up from beneath craggy brows

she transferred her gaze to him

he sat on the edge of the desk looking down at her

he cast an approving glance at her tanned thighs

for an instant his glance sharpened

unseeing, she stared past them all

he measured her with a cool appraising look

he stared back in waiting silence

for a long moment, she looked back at him

she took a frank and admiring look at him

she studied his face unhurriedly, feature by feature

he turned around to look directly at her

he glanced sideways in surprise

they exchanged a subtle look of amusement

Other

his eyes were hooded like those of a hawk

her dark, earnest eyes sought his

his eyes darkened dangerously

for a moment he studied her intently

his eyes studying her with a curious intensity

seeing the gleam of interest in his eyes

a probing query came into his eyes

his eyes drank her up

his eyes alone betrayed his ardor

his eyes seemed to undress her

his eyes darkened with emotion

there was an invitation in the smoldering depths of his eyes

she was enthralled by what she saw

his quick gray eyes were humorous and tender

her eyes were pools of appeal

his eyes bathed her in admiration

her eyes told him everything she felt

the light of desire illuminated his mellow blue eyes

her eyes shimmered with the light from the window

he made passionate love to her with his eyes

her dark eyes reflected glimmers of light

his eyes sent her a private message

she tried to relax, but he held her eyes

she saw him out of the tail of her eye

her eyes clouded with visions of the past

her eyes froze on his lips

she could feel his sharp eyes boring into her as she walked away

it took several seconds for her eyes to adjust

her eyes drank in the sensuality of his physique

her eyes took in his powerful presence

his eyes were as dark and powerful as he was

the fringe of her lashes cast shadows on her cheeks

his glance was bemused and opaque

she glanced at his well-defined profile

he stared at her with rounded eyes

she couldn't resist another glance at him

she stared at the twinkling lights

pausing, he gazed at her speculatively

she stole a glance at his face

she regarded him with a speculative gaze

she glanced up at him, but he didn't give her a chance to answer

there was something lazily seductive in his look

he glanced at her for a sign of objection

she looked at him quickly, hopefully

she regarded him with impassive coldness

his gaze came to rest on her questioning eyes

he studied her thoughtfully for a moment

she found a joyous satisfaction in studying his profile

she watched the play of emotions on his face

she looked in the mirror, studying herself disapprovingly

he surveyed the road judiciously

Voices

Types, Characteristics of Speech

his voice was resigned

he spoke in an odd, yet gentle tone

she answered quickly over her choking, beating heart

he spoke in a tone filled with awe and respect

he said with quiet emphasis

a tear-smothered voice whispered behind her

he answered with staid calmness

she spoke eagerly

his voice was courteous but patronizing

he had a mild, interested voice

her voice was fragile and shaking

he repeated in the same cool tone

he said in a grudging voice

she heard his voice, chuckling and hearty

he answered indulgently

she muttered hastily

her voice rang with command

his tone was apologetic

she spoke with as reasonable a voice as she could manage

his soothing voice probed further

his voice had an infinitely compassionate tone

there was a gentle softness in her voice

she had no idea how sensuous her voice sounded

the huskiness lingered in his tone

his voice lulled her into a relaxed mood

the underlying sensuality of his words captivated her

she spoke in a weak and tremulous whisper

his tone was irascibly patient

the intensity in her lowered voice

she said in a silky voice

his voice was resonant and impressive

he was whistling softly

she could hardly lift her voice above a whisper

he said matter-of-factly

her voice sounded tired

his voice broke with huskiness

she said firmly

her voice broke

she spoke in a broken whisper

his voice was calm, his gaze steady

his hoarse whisper broke the silence

the voice was velvet-edged and strong

his voice was smooth, but insistent

his voice, deep and sensual, sent a ripple of awareness through her

she spoke in a suffocated whisper

his voice carried a unique force

his voice was soothing, yet oddly disconcerting

her reply lacked a ring of finality

she heard his full and masculine laugh

his voice was thick and unsteady

his silky voice held a challenge

he commented as if the answer were obvious

his voice was uncompromising yet oddly gentle

her voice was full of entreaty

he asked with deceptive calm

his voice had depth and authority

there was a trace of laughter in his voice

she blurted, scarcely aware of her own voice

he added with mock severity

there was a faint tremor in his voice as though some emotion had touched him

his voice held a rasp of excitement

he broke off then with an apology

there was a slight tinge of wonder in his voice

the soft voice urged her

he spoke with cool authority

she detected a thawing in his tone

his tone had a degree of warmth and concern

his words were as cool and clear as ice water

she whispered, her hand on her breast

he said the words with the certainty of a man who could never be satisfied with only a dream

recovering, he said lightly

he asked again, and this time his voice was more friendly

when he spoke again his voice was warm

her voice was shakier than she would have liked

she heard her voice, stifled and unnatural

when he spoke again, his voice was tender, almost a murmur

fortunately, no one noticed the tremor in her voice

his stammering voice was only a buzz in her ear

her voice was like silken oak

his voice was distant

she said softly, her eyes narrowing

his voice, though deep, was crisp and clear

he replied without inflection

his cool voice broke into her reverie

her throaty voice

she had a wonderful low voice, soft and clear

she said in a voice that seemed to come from a long way off

his voice was low and smooth

his greeting was a husky whisper

a male voice cut through her thoughts

his voice was a velvet murmur

her voice was deep and dusty

managing no more than a hoarse whisper

he announced in boarding-school English

the rich timbre of his voice

his voice echoed her own longings

he spoke freely about what he was thinking

she responded matter-of-factly

his voice was soft but alarming

she had a low, silvery voice

his deep-timbred voice

he said in a deep tone

his voice was low and purposefully seductive

his low voice was a little awkward

he said in a low, composed voice

his deep voice simmered with barely checked passion

his mellow baritone was edged with control

Negative Responses

an exasperated male voice drifted into the foyer where she was waiting

his greeting contained a strong suggestion of reproach

his voice was heavy with sarcasm

his voice hardened ruthlessly

a silken thread of warning in his voice

he said softly, mockingly

his tone was coolly disapproving

his voice was rough with anxiety

his voice was stern with no vestige of sympathy in its hardness

he had a possessive desperation in his voice

his words seemed worn, thin and hollow, used so often by shallow men

she didn't fail to catch the note of sarcasm in his voice

he warned half seriously

he ground the word out between his teeth

his voice was almost an affront to the silence

his contemptuous tone sparked her anger

his voice was cold and exact

he asked, spacing the words evenly

a voice cut the silence

his tone was velvet, yet edged with steel

she remarked, pleased at how nonchalant she sounded

there was an edge to his voice

her tone had become chilly

the words were playful but the meaning was not

he murmured satirically

he said in his usual discontented voice

he sighed with exasperation

his voice, though quiet, had an ominous quality

he answered in a tense, clipped voice that forbade any questions

he said in a dull and troubled voice

his words were loaded with ridicule

in spite of her reserve a tinge of exasperation came into her voice

he said tersely

his voice hardened

she said in a choked voice

he said in a harsh, raw voice

she spoke with light bitterness

he spoke without a hint of boastfulness

as her tone hardened, she retorted tartly

she showed her disbelief in the tone of her voice

she heard her bitterness spill over into her voice

there was a bitter edge of cynicism in his voice

his coolly impersonal tone broke the stillness

his voice grated harshly

there was a cold edge of irony in his voice

he said in a nasty tone

his voice was like an echo from an empty tomb

he insisted archly

he answered with his facile tongue

she demanded in a shrill voice

Other

she lowered her voice, being purposefully mysterious

her voice faded to a hushed stillness

her voice died away

he added, in a lower, huskier tone

he leaned forward and lowered his voice

his voice dropped in volume

his voice faded, losing its steely edge

her voice rose an octave

at the sound of his voice, she lifted her head and listened

she spoke loudly and the words seemed strange on her tongue

the raucous sounds of laughter and snatches of song filled the night air

he spoke to all, but gazed only at her

he let out a long, audible breath

Emotions

Happiness, Joy

joy bubbled in her laugh and shone in her eyes
even her walk had a sunny cheerfulness
he exclaimed with intense pleasure
he exhaled a long sigh of contentment
his presence gave her joy
her smile broadened in approval
satisfaction pursed her mouth
she felt a bottomless peace and satisfaction
her features became more animated
tonight there were no shadows across her heart
a part of her reveled in his open admiration of her
her heart sang with delight
she was blissfully happy, fully alive
she felt a warm glow flow through her
she gloried briefly in the shared moment

she was wrapped in a silken cocoon of euphoria

his mood seemed suddenly buoyant

he pressed her with relentless enjoyment

a cry of relief broke from her lips

Confidence

she basked in the knowledge of her power

she watched with smug delight

an expression of satisfaction showed in her eyes

she straightened herself with dignity

his touch was reassuring

she was impressed with the obvious confidence he inspired

she felt as if her dormant wits had renewed themselves

as the words began to flow, she gathered her strength

a sense of strength came to her and her despair lessened

her newly awakened sense of life comforted her

powerful relief filled her

her defenses began to subside

at this point, she was beyond intimidation

she felt elated by her new objectivity

tragedy had etched composure and dignity into her face

she forced remote dignity into her voice

tears were gone, as if evaporated by an onrushing wind

she saw him with abrupt clarity

she was certain now that she was in love with him

she'd proven adept at handling herself

he felt a strange numbed comfort

he had an indefinable feeling of rightness

she felt no burdensome chains of involvement

with a pulse-pounding certainty she knew

her body vibrated with new life

she had an air of calm and self-confidence which he liked

her confidence spiraled upward

he was sure of himself and his rightful place in the universe

he seemed very pleased with himself

he took charge with quiet assurance

confidently, she rejected such an idea as absurd

Determination

---

her face was full of strength, shining with a steadfast and serene peace

she resolved to let her trip revitalize her senses

with dazzling determination

her courage and determination were like a rock inside her

he seemed to enjoy her struggle to capture her composure

there was still a chance for her to grow whole again

her lips were pressed shut so no sound would burst out

she forced herself to settle down

she vowed to show him how unconcerned she was

she spoke with quiet, but desperate, firmness

she studiously avoided his presence

she was determined not to reveal her joy at seeing him

she kept all expression from her voice when she apologized

she imposed an iron control on herself

he showed no signs of relenting

she was determined to straighten the havoc alone

she bit her lip to stifle the outcry

determined, she grimly set about building a new life for herself

she clenched her jaw to kill the sob in her throat

she tried to maintain her curtness

she struggled to maintain an even, conciliatory tone

her determination faltered

she fought hard against the tears she refused to let fall

she proved to herself that she was immune to him

she had no intention of permitting herself to fall under the spell

she fought the dynamic vitality he exuded

she couldn't afford to be distracted by romantic notions

girding herself with resolve

after a long pause, during which she fought for self-control, she demanded

she drew a deep breath and forbade herself to tremble

she clung to reality, praying she would not betray her agitation

she quickly waved aside his hesitation

his voice was firm, final

with the sense of conviction that was part of her character

pride kept her from arguing

she took a deep breath punctuated with several even gasps

she forced her lips to part in a curved, stiff smile

Defiance

she added with a slight smile of defiance

he waited, challenging her to go through with it

finally she managed to pierce his complacency

she lifted her chin, meeting his icy gaze straight on

she threw back her head and placed her hands on her hips

tossing her hair across her shoulders in a gesture of defiance

she swallowed hard, lifted her chin, and boldly met his gaze

she boldly met his eyes

the outcry unleashed something within her

she ordered in a voice of authority

she responded sharply, abandoning all pretense

she resisted with every means in her power

she stiffened at the challenge

she found a perverse pleasure in the challenge

his hands placed belligerently on his hips

triumph flooded through her when he winced at her words

she met his accusing eyes without flinching

she tossed her head and eyed him with cold triumph

she would not let herself be put down by this brute

every curve of her body spoke defiance

she answered in a rush of words

there was defiance in her tone as well as subtle challenge

she said, with easy defiance

she plunged on carelessly

she moved without haste, but with unhurried purpose

she pretended not to understand his look

Surprise

she became instantly wide awake

she was too startled by his suggestion to offer any objection

the heavy lashes that shadowed her cheeks flew up

she stood up, surprised, and more uncertain than ever

she said, clearly surprised that he had asked her

intense astonishment touched her pale face

to her interested amazement

the shock of discovery hit her full force

she was caught off guard by the sudden vibrancy of his voice

she said, surprised again by this unpredictable man

she was shocked when his eyes suddenly filled with fierce sparkling

she merely stared, tongue-tied

she stood there, blank, amazed, and very shaken

she heard his quick intake of breath

she halted, shocked

the girl looked at her in surprise

a soft gasp escaped her

surprise siphoned the blood from her face

she was too surprised to do more than nod

the tenderness in his expression amazed her

her mouth dropped open

she started, realizing he was not what she thought

she was too stunned to cry

she exclaimed, amazed at the constant diversions

startled at her own voice, she glanced up

she jumped at the sound of his voice

she looked at him with surprise, remembering his hostility

he was an ever-changing mystery

they both froze in a stunned tableau

she snapped her mouth shut, stunned by his bluntness

she took a quick sharp breath

through the roaring din, she breathed one word

she stared, wordlessly

he gave her a sidelong glance of utter disbelief

she stared wordlessly across at him, her heart pounding

she was stunned by his cool appraisal

a new and unexpected warmth surged through her

she was amazed at the thrill he gave her

shock flew through her

her body stiffened in shock

the shock caused the words to wedge in her throat

his astonishment was obviously genuine and she regretted her jibe

as their eyes met, she felt a shock run through her

more surprised than frightened, she looked up

he was momentarily speechless in his surprise

her voice rose in surprise

her jade-spoked eyes widened with astonishment

she was barely able to control her gasp of surprise

to her surprise, he showed no reaction

he stared, complete surprise on his face

she took a quick breath of utter astonishment

her voice broke off in midsentence

her breath caught in her lungs

she stared, speechless

she couldn't rally quick enough to protest

she stared at him in astonishment

his luminous eyes widened in astonishment

wave after wave of shock slapped at her

Annoyance, Irritation

she was irked by his cool, aloof manner

she was both excited and aggravated

he insisted with returning impatience

she felt restless and irritable

her voice was hoarse with frustration

she felt irritable and unhappy with herself

she tried to disguise her annoyance in front of the others

with both hands on her hips, she confronted him

she turned away without waiting for a reply

irritated by his mocking tone

she retorted in cold sarcasm

he gave her a black layered look

he replied with heavy irony

there was a critical tone to his voice

he ripped out the words impatiently

he retained his affability, but there was a distinct hardening of his eyes she bit down hard on her lower lip

with a vague hint of disapproval

her coolness was evidence that she was not amused

he sounded curt, abstracted

he drawled with distinct mockery

accentuating the annoyance she felt with herself

she exclaimed with a twinge of envy

with unwelcome frankness

to her annoyance, she found herself starting to blush

his lips puckered with annoyance

she was annoyed at the transparency of her feelings

a suggestion of annoyance hovered in his eyes

she detected a hint of censure in his tone

she laughed to cover her annoyance

his vexation was evident

he stiffened as though she had struck him

a shadow of annoyance crossed his face

he gritted his teeth

he clenched his mouth tighter

she found herself inexplicably dissatisfied

she exclaimed in irritation as she jumped to her feet

his response held a note of impatience

she heard a heavy dose of sarcasm in his voice

her annoyance increased when she found that her hands were shaking

his tongue was heavy with sarcasm

aware of her annoyance, he tried to coax her into a better mood

the cynicism of the remark grated on her

she quickly chastised herself

his mouth was set in annoyance

she was generally resentful of the situation

the corner of his mouth twisted with exasperation

her lips thinned with irritation

he whispered harshly and gave her a little shake

she was irritated at the thrilling current moving through her

his eyes met hers disparagingly

her lower lip trembled as she returned his glare

his straight glance seemed to be accusing her coldly

a bright mockery invaded his stare

he shot her a penetrating look as she rose

his stare drilled into her

he glared at her, frowning

now she was the victim of his glare

he gave her a brutal and unfriendly stare

there was derision and sympathy mingled in his glance

they stared at each other across a sudden ringing silence

from lowered lids, she shot a commanding look at him

his gray eyes darkened as he held her gaze

his accusing gaze was riveted on her

his glare burned through her

she reflected with some bitterness

Confusion

she shrugged to hide her confusion

all of her loneliness and confusion welded together in one upsurge of devouring yearning

she had to conquer her involuntary reactions to that gentle loving look of his

his dark eyes showed the tortured dullness of disbelief

she fought through the cobwebs of nightmare-filled sleep

she looked up, disoriented

when he switched all that intensity to her, she became confused

she found him vaguely disturbing

then why should she agonize over it?

half in anticipation, half in dread

disconcerted, she crossed her arms and pointedly looked away

confused, she wandered restlessly around the room

it was hard to remain coherent when so close to him

it sent her pulses spinning

in dazed exasperation

she hesitated, blinking with bafflement

she listened with bewilderment

she hesitated, torn by conflicting emotions

she felt the screams of frustration at the back of her throat

she experienced a gamut of perplexing emotions

her bearing was stiff and proud, but her spirit was in chaos

she sat back, momentarily rebuffed

distraction was evident in her every move

she tried weighing the whole structure of events

she was swimming through a haze of feelings and desires

she was frozen in limbo where all decisions and actions were impossible

a faint thread of hysteria was back in her voice

a slight hesitation in his hawklike eyes

she found his nearness disturbing and exciting

some of her anger evaporated, leaving only confusion

she lowered her gaze in confusion

she wanted to hurt him and to make him want her at the same time

tormented by confusing emotions

the future looked vague and shadowy

welcoming the confusion, she took the moment to catch her breath

her ironic tone concealed the mixed emotions she felt

she was so confused and badgered she couldn't speak

her pride concealed her inner turmoil

her mind was spinning with bewilderment

her mind whirled at his dry response

he stared at her, baffled

she was totally bewildered at his behavior

a tumble of confused thoughts and feelings assailed her

she heard sounds, muted and sharp at the same time

she found herself responding to his harsh features despite herself

her mind refused to register the significance of his words

she was confused by her unexpected response to his touch

mixed feelings surged through her

she tried to force her confused emotions into order

she masked her inner turmoil with a deceptive calmness

she fought to control her swirling emotions

a war of emotions raged within her

she was sick with the struggle within her

she was baffled by his stern attitude

she was puzzled by his abrupt change in mood

his words didn't register on her dizzied senses

she was unwilling to face him and unable to turn away

her brain was in tumult

her feelings toward him were becoming confused

her troubled spirits quieted

her mind reeled with confusion

her emotions seemed out of control

strange and disquieting thoughts began to race through her mind

she wavered, trying to comprehend what she was hearing

after a long and troubled night of soul searching

her head swirled with doubts

what had happened to the level-headed young woman of yesterday?

she was too concerned with her response to offer a reply

under his steady scrutiny, she couldn't think

with difficulty she struggled back to wakefulness

she closed the door and her mind

her mind was working overtime again

she was more shaken than she cared to admit

he was a complex man, not easy to know intimately

she needed a moment to reorient herself

her heart refused to believe what her mind told her

it was as if he was trying to draw a response from her

he faltered in the silence that engulfed them

she wondered if she should confess her doubts to him

she was unnerved by the sudden change

her thoughts scampered vaguely around

she was puzzled and more than a little nervous

Fear, Anxiety, Tension

---

fear and anger knotted inside her

the ferocity of his passion was frightening as well as exalting

fear, stark and vivid, glittered in her eyes

she gasped, realizing a shiver of panic

sheer black fright swept through her

she began to shake as the fearful images built in her mind

a quick and disturbing thought

just thinking of it shattered her
the thought tore at her insides
she searched anxiously for the meaning behind the words
the question was a stab in her heart
his voice was absolutely emotionless and it chilled her
she replied in a small frightened voice
icy fear twisted around her heart
sounds gushed in from the hallway, battering her
she felt disturbing quakes in her serenity
she tried to keep her fragile control
her stomach was still clenched tight
it was impossible to steady her erratic pulse
her mind a crazy mixture of hope and fear
she seemed to be more afraid of herself than of him
panic like she'd never known before welled in her throat
she gasped, panting in terror
but her fears were premature
a flicker of apprehension coursed through her
anxiety cooled her thoughts
in her heart she had always been afraid
she felt momentary panic as her mind jumped on
a wave of apprehension swept through her
it gnawed away at her confidence
in ways that alternately thrilled and frightened her
the strange surge of affection she felt frightened her
panic was rioting within her

she came to an abrupt stop, her heart jumping in her chest

despite her fears, she felt a hot and awful joy

she felt impaled by his steady gaze

she choked back a cry, frightened, electrified

but the relief was short-lived

she watched with acute and loving anxiety

a thrill of frightened anticipation touched her spine

she tried to keep her heart cold and still

her pulse began to beat erratically at the threatening in his deep voice

she felt as if her breath was cut off

her mind fluttered away in anxiety

anxiety spurted through her

her stomach churning with anxiety and frustration

half in anticipation, half in dread

he seemed relieved to be released from the conversation

she sought to erect a wall of defense against him

the tension between them increased with frightening intensity

the silence lengthened between them, making her uncomfortable

a chill black silence surrounded them

a tense silence enveloped the room

the tension between them began to melt

a volcano on the verge of erupting

she gave in to the tension that had been building all day

silence grew tight with tension

there remained a certain tension in his attitude

there was a long, brittle silence

the silence loomed between them like a heavy mist

there was tension among the people in the room

her spirits were out of tempo with the tense drawn face that greeted her

the unwelcome tension stretched ever tighter between them

as if holding a raw emotion in check

she breathed in shallow, quick gasps

her chest felt as if it would burst

the tense lines on her face relaxed

the chill between them seemed to grow

a cold knot formed in her stomach

her nerves tensed immediately

the tension was gone from her face when she turned to him

a pulsing knot within her demanded more

the tight knot within her begged for release

her breath seemed to have solidified in her throat

she felt as if a hand had closed around her throat

she couldn't control the spasmodic trembling within her

she'd been more tense than she'd thought

the muscles of his forearm hardened beneath the sleeve

she clenched her hand until her nails entered her palm

the anxious look on her face told her he knew

his expression darkened with an unreadable emotion

her heart was thumping madly as she punched the doorbell

she huddled in her chair, making no response

she noticed his unresponsiveness

the color drained from her face

with a pang, she realized

she gave an anxious little cough

she took a deep breath and tried to relax

nervously, she bit her lip

she swallowed with difficulty and found her voice

she felt a terrible tenseness in her body

Caution, Insecurity, Uneasiness

biting her lip, she looked away

as casually as she could manage, she asked

there was a pensive shimmer in the shadow of her eyes

she felt her composure was under attack

she was suddenly anxious to escape from his disturbing presence

she sat in the chair, her thin fingers tensed in her lap

she stammered in bewilderment

she became increasingly uneasy under his scrutiny

awkwardly, she cleared her throat

she looked away hastily, then moved restlessly

she caught herself glancing uneasily over her shoulder

she floundered before the brilliance of his look

uncertainty made her voice harsh and demanding

to her dismay, her voice broke slightly

perhaps it was simply her own uneasiness

when she tried to speak, her voice wavered

she muttered uneasily

searching for a plausible explanation

her thoughts were dull and disquieting

she stirred uneasily in the chair

she was uncomfortable with the fact that he'd spoken the truth

her face clouded with uneasiness

she became more uncomfortable by the minute as her dismay grew

a warning voice whispered in her head

she flinched at the tone of his voice

she only half listened as she struggled with her conscience

he aroused old fears and uncertainties

she swallowed hard, trying to manage a feeble answer

she had a much stronger guard up now

her voice had drifted into a hushed whisper

she hated to admit how much his admiration cheered her

he said the words tentatively as if testing the idea

that alone set alarm bells ringing

she hoped her smile was noncommittal

her composure was a fragile shell around her

at least there'd be no disturbing surprises

her hands, hidden from sight, twisted nervously in her lap

he hesitated, measuring her for a moment

she sensed his disquiet

all her nervousness slipped back to grip her

the amusement died from her eyes and she regarded him with searching gravity

a shadow of alarm touched her face

he gave her a narrowed glinting glance

her sleep had been interrupted periodically by anticipation

she depicted an ease she didn't necessarily feel

not so, her heart whispered back

she watched him warily as he sat down

something cautioned her not to ask

she chewed on her lower lip and stole a look at him

she was uncomfortable with his ability to figure her out

unfamiliar sounds seeped in to haunt her

her mind was congested with doubts and fears

something disturbing replaced his smoldering look

only now that he was gone did she dare to relax

she chose her words carefully

his voice was carefully colored in neutral shades

she had to sheath her inner feelings

something was flickering far back in her eyes

as she paused to catch her breath, her fears were stronger than ever

her misgivings increased by the minute

his face closed, as if guarding a secret

she was halted by the tone of his voice

she felt suddenly ill-equipped to undertake such a task

she felt herself shrinking from the cold gray of his watchful smile

an oddly primitive warning sounded in her brain

his distrust chilled his eyes with reserve

she stood slumped over with a worried expression

she flinched and retreated a step before his expression

she looked up at him with an effort

her relief altered instantly into suspicion

the nagging in the back of her mind refused to be stilled

she would have to guard her own actions as well as his

warning spasms of alarm erupted within her

every fiber in her body warned her against him

her breath caught in her throat as she felt her heart pounding

she struggled with the uncertainty that had been aroused

some sixth sense brought her fully awake

she turned away, wearied by indecision

he regarded her quizzically for a moment

a sense of inadequacy swept over her

she doubted he was a man of delicate scruples

an uncertainty crept into his expression

he said with detached inevitability

his mind floundered

Anger, Rage

she glared at him with burning, reproachful eyes

his temper when crossed could be almost uncontrollable

fury almost choked her

her mood veered sharply to anger

he had not missed her flare of temper

the bridled anger in his voice

curses fell from his mouth

he shook her into gasping silence

he didn't care whether he hurt her or not

his expression clouded in anger

she gave him a hostile glare

she spat out the words contemptuously

her temper flared

his anger became a scalding fury

sudden anger lit her eyes

she permitted herself a withering stare

his laugh raked her

he replied sharply

her green eyes clawed him like talons

his curt voice lashed at her

he repeated with contempt

she seethed with anger and humiliation

clenching her teeth, she was furious

she threw the words at him like stones

she was breathless with rage

she swallowed hard, trying not to reveal her anger

rancor sharpened her voice

she seethed with mounting rage

his tone aroused and infuriated her

he interrupted her vehemently

the angry retort hardened his features

her eyes conveyed the fury within her

his face was a glowering mask of rage

her anger abated somewhat under the warm glow of his smile

he glowered at her and turned away

he looked at her with a sardonic expression that sent her temper soaring

she was furious at her vulnerability to him

a sudden thin chill hung on the edge of his words

she reacted angrily to the challenge in his voice

shock yielded quickly to fury

she felt suddenly weak and vulnerable in the face of his anger

her lips thinned with anger

her nostrils flared with fury

the lively twinkle in his eye only incensed her more

hardening her heart by erecting barriers of anger
she licked her lower lip, managing to quell her anger
his chiding tone made her angry
her features contorted with shock and anger
she was staring with haughty rebuke
she flashed him a look of disdain
his tone was relatively civil in spite of his anger
startled hurt turned into white-hot anger
he replied in reckless anger
she felt her temper rise in response
choking on her own words
the insolence in her voice was ill-concealed
her accusing voice stabbed the air
her rebellious emotions got out of hand
his expression bordered on mockery
she shot him a cold look
he chuckled nastily
she countered icily
denial flew from her
cold eyes sniped at her
the force of his seething reply took her off guard
his voice was cold when he answered
he whirled to stare at her, quick anger rising in his eyes
his eyes blazed amber fire
she was numb with increasing rage and shock
his broad-carved face twisted in anger

a swift shadow of anger swept across her face

his voice was cold and lashing

she shook with impotent rage and fear

each assessed the other's anger

shock and anger lit up her eyes as she turned to face him

she suppressed her anger under the appearance of indifference

he replied with contempt that forbade any further argument

her breath came raggedly in impotent anger

his voice was inflamed and belligerent

her expression was thunderous

struggling free, her blue eyes blazing, she faced him furiously

she was so furious she could hardly speak

he had a fiery, angry look that was unfamiliar to her

her face paled with anger

his voice was quiet, yet held an undertone of cold contempt

she sputtered, bristling with indignation

she replied in a low voice, taut with anger

his eyes were black and dazzling with fury

he stood there, tall and angry

the long deep look they exchanged infuriated her

her breath burned in her throat

she suddenly paled with wrath

her gray eyes darkened like angry thunderclouds

his angry gaze swung over her

again anger singed the corners of her control

her own anger and hurt could no longer be controlled

he shook his head vehemently

he tempered his anger with amusement

alarm and anger rippled along her spine

her heart was hammering, her breathing ragged

he glanced sharply round, his eyes blazing

his whole demeanor was growing in severity

the silence between them became unbearable

her thoughts were racing dangerously

Humiliation, Embarrassment

she colored fiercely

the blood began to pound in her temples

she stiffened, momentarily abashed

stains of scarlet appeared on her cheeks

she was glad of the semidarkness that hid the flush in her cheeks

it was a humiliating, deflated feeling

an unwelcome blush crept into her cheeks

her cheeks burned in remembrance

she saw his eyes, large glittering ovals of repudiation

her breath quickened, her cheeks became warm

she detected a condescension in his attitude

she was crimson with resentment and humiliation

with renewed humiliation, she looked away

her pride had been seriously bruised by his behavior

she was intensely humiliated

she turned a vivid scarlet

his florid, self-satisfied face mocked her

heat stealing into her face

his caustic tone made her flush in shame

she paled at the enormity of the command

she was filled with humiliation

her embarrassment turned to raw fury

among other emotions was a deep sense of shame

the flush receded, leaving two red spots on her white cheeks

she felt a shudder of humiliation

she was almost embarrassed at how happy that made her

the embarrassment quickly turned to annoyance

her face was flushed with humiliation and anger at herself

her flush deepened to crimson

she was angry at herself for being embarrassed

she was helpless to halt her embarrassment

she flushed miserably

her blood pounded, her face grew hot with humiliation

she was humiliatingly conscious of his scrutiny

a blush like a shadow ran over her cheeks

she attempted to ease his embarrassment and hers as well

her humiliation could not be alleviated

mercifully, the moonlight hid the extent of her embarrassment

she blushed at her own excitement

she buried her burning face against his shoulder

she was ashamed at having taken advantage of his trusting nature

Despair, Anguish, Defeat

she shuddered inwardly at the thought

she had seen too much, witnessed too many painful scenes

she needed more time to erase the pain

she felt ice spreading through her stomach

she felt an acute sense of loss

she floundered in an agonizing maelstrom

she shriveled a little at his expression

she couldn't accept the dull ache of foreboding

her misery was so acute that it was a physical pain

terrible regrets assailed her

her misery was like a steel weight

she bit her lip until it throbbed like her pulse

her anguish almost overcoming her control

a glazed look of despair began to spread over her face

she felt the nauseating sinking of despair

she gave a choked, desperate laugh

the torment of his presence

her expression was one of mute wretchedness

she swallowed the despair in her throat

she replied in a low, tormented voice

how desperately she needed him, clung to him

her anguish peaked to shatter the last shreds of her control

a raw and primitive grief overwhelmed her

she shrugged in mock resignation

she wrapped herself in a cocoon of anguish

she pressed her hand over her face convulsively

her throat ached with defeat

her energies were wasted against his granite stand

she felt a wretchedness of mind she'd never known before

the shock of defeat held her immobile

a stab of guilt lay buried in her breast

he was pleased to hear her admit her weaknesses

trapped in her own lie, she was defeated

she was assailed by a terrible sense of bitterness

she felt bereft and desolate

her mind was languid, without hope

in work she found a mindless solidity that helped camouflage the deep despair of loneliness swallowing the sob that rose in her throat, she looked up

stunned and sickened, she repeated what he said

his thoughts tasted like gall

the endless night finally grayed into dawn

the hurt and longing lay naked in her eyes

her spirits sank even lower

her head was bowed, her body slumped in despair

she couldn't bear the sight of him without breaking down herself

she closed her eyes, feeling utterly miserable

grief and despair tore at her heart

a sensation of intense sickness and desolation swept over her

she was silent and defeated

finally, in desperation, she called to him

she flung out her hands in simple despair

a bitter cold despair dwelt in the caves of her lonely soul

she faced a lightless future

her eyes darkened with pain

his hands shoved in his pockets, his shoulders hunched forward

he sighed heavily, his voice filled with anguish

she closed her eyes, her heart aching with pain

a flash of loneliness stabbed at her

a new anguish seared her heart

she covered her face with trembling hands and gave vent to the agony of her loss the pain in her heart became a sick and fiery gnawing

she felt icy fingers seep into every pore

her teeth chattered, her body trembled

an inner torment began to gnaw at her

torment was eating at her from the inside

he spoke so viciously that she wondered how she could ever have thought him kind

a deep, unaccustomed pain in her breast

the spark of hope quickly extinguished

she gazed at him in despair

she was a woman facing the harsh realities of loneliness

she sighed, then gave a resigned shrug

her mouth opened in dismay

a suffocating sensation tightened her throat

again she was assaulted by her sick yearning

her throat was raw with unuttered shouts and protests

she felt guilty and selfish

his expression was grim as he watched her

a bitter jealousy stirred inside him

the knowledge twisted and turned inside her

his expression was like someone who had been struck in the face

she felt him shudder as he drew in a sharp breath

his broad shoulders were heaving as he breathed

she was suddenly overwhelmed by the torment of the past few weeks

the insults were barbed and hurtful

the swell of pain was beyond tears

his face was bleak with sorrow

she tried to hide her inner misery from his probing stare

the effect on her was shattering

he had sliced open a newly healed wound

there was a heavy feeling in her stomach

her heart squeezed in anguish as she realized

it was sinking anguish which caused her to stumble

she closed her eyes, reliving the pain of that final scene

her stomach knotted and she stiffened under his withering glare

she was actually trembling now

the offending hands gripped her upper arms

she could feel her throat closing up

it was senselessly and sickeningly familiar

her mouth felt like old paper, dry and dusty

with a moan of distress, she turned away

her throat seemed to close up

the last traces of resistance vanished

he had broken through her fragile control

she had walked into it with her heart wide open

her breasts rose and fell under her labored breathing

her breath was shallow, her senses drugged

she took deep breaths until she was strong enough to raise her head

little by little, warmth crept back into her body

she wasn't up to coping
it was pointless to deny his attraction for her

Tears

tears blinding her eyes and choking her voice
tears glistened on her pale, heart-shaped face
tears still trembled on her eyelids
she stained the book with her tears
he was seemingly unmoved by her sobs
she wept aloud, rocking back and forth
a hot exultant tear trickling down her cheek
smothering a sob, she fled
a hot tear rolled down her cheek
she gulped hard, hot tears slipping down her cheeks
her eyes were bordered with tears
she held back tears of disappointment
deep sobs racked her insides
tears slowly found their way down her cheeks
her tears choked her
she yielded to the compulsive sobs that shook her
she was conscious only of a low, tortured sob
she tore herself away with a choking cry
she rigidly held her tears in check
she swallowed hard and bit back tears

biting her lips to control the sobs

brushing away tears to see, she opened the letter

her clamped lips imprisoned a sob

tears welled within her eyes

tears of pleasure found their way to her eyes

her gaze was clouded with tears

her eyes filled with tears of frustration

she wept aloud, rocking back and forth

the tears were the result of pure nostalgia

Unhappiness, Disappointment

with an odd twinge of disappointment

a flash of wild grief ripped through her

her sorrow was a huge, painful knot inside

her mouth was as pale as her cheeks

her vow weighed upon her, choking her

quiet, withdrawn, and worried

her thoughts, jagged and painful

her voice broke miserably

when she lifted her eyes, the pain still flickered there

her life had become a bitter battle

suddenly all pleasure left her

the misery of the night still haunted her

her sense of loss was beyond tears

the only things left were the raw sores of an aching heart

her own feelings were still too raw to discuss

she sensed an odd twinge of disappointment

a permanent sorrow seemed to weigh her down

she listened with rising dismay

her vision was still gloomily colored with the memory

a heaviness centered in her chest

there was a sourness in the pit of her stomach

like an old wound that ached on a rainy day

she paused and continued in sinking tones

she sighed, clasped her slender hands together, and stared at them

she dropped her lashes quickly to hide the hurt

she heard his voice and bit her lips in dismay

he shook his head regretfully

leaving her with an inexplicable feeling of emptiness

his short bark of humor lacked laughter

she settled back, disappointed

added to her disappointment was a feeling of guilt

she answered him thickly

she stopped short in dismay

he seemed disappointed at her hesitation

she spoke calmly, with no lighting of her eyes, no smile of tenderness

the animation left her face

she ached with an inner pain

a pain squeezed her heart as she thought of him
she sat in lonely silence
she felt an instant's squeezing hurt
trying to swallow the lump that lingered in her throat
a look of tired sadness passed over her features
her glowing youthful happiness faded
he hadn't noticed the strained tone of her voice

Sex

Desire, Attraction

a vaguely sensuous light passed between them

she was strangely flattered by his interest

carried away by her own response, she failed to notice

her whole being seemed to be filled with waiting

when she saw him her only emotion was relief

the prolonged anticipation was almost unbearable

a sense of urgency drove her

she felt an eager affection coming from him

she could feel the sexual magnetism that made him so self-confident

she saw the heart rending tenderness of his gaze

he looked her over seductively

he seemed to be peering at her intently

she stared with longing at him

every time his gaze met hers, her heart turned over in response he looked at her as if he were photographing her with his eyes

he scanned her critically and beamed approval

his glance slid rapidly to her bathing suit and his mouth softened

his eyes raked boldly over her

his gaze dropped from her eyes to her shoulders to her breasts

his stare was bold and assessed her frankly

slowly and seductively, his gaze slid downward

he gave her body a raking gaze

his gaze roved and lazily appraised her

his gaze fell to the creamy expanse of her neck

she noticed he was watching her intently

he looked at her and the double meaning of his gaze was very obvious

his gaze was as soft as a caress

his steady gaze bore into her in silent expectation

his gaze traveled over her face and searched her eyes

his gaze was riveted on her face, then moved over her body slowly

something intense flared through his entrancement

she had to fight her overwhelming need to be close to him

there was a tingling in the pit of her stomach

her heart jolted and her pulse pounded

he was so disturbing to her in every way

she tried to throttle the dizzying current racing through her

she was by no means blind to his attraction

her curiosity, as well as her vanity, was aroused

he radiated a vitality that drew her like a magnet

he was as eager and erratic as a summer storm

there was an air of efficiency about him that fascinated her

something in his manner soothed her

there was a maddening hint of arrogance about him

her body ached for his touch

she dreamed of being crushed within his embrace

he had unlocked her heart and soul

she didn't miss his obvious examination and approval

every day, her love deepened and intensified

such an attraction would be perilous

he stoked a gently growing fire

the smoldering flame she saw in his eyes startled her

the idea sent her spirits soaring

she was pleased with their initial intimacy

she replied with complacent buoyancy

happiness filled her as she talked

she tried to learn him by heart

her feet seemed to be drifting along on a cloud

she found herself extremely conscious of his virile appeal

she was powerless to resist

each time she saw him, the pull was stronger
she admired his driving intelligence
she felt a ripple of excitement
her interest stirred at their introduction
her attention perked up at the mention of him
there was a deeper significance to the visual interchange
his appeal was devastating
the very air around her seemed electrified
her heart danced with excitement
she felt a lurch of excitement within her
the implication sent waves of excitement through her
she felt an unwelcome surge of excitement
a slender delicate thread began to form between them
she drank in the comfort of his nearness
the sound of his voice affected her deeply
her heart ached under her breast
her insides jangled with excitement
it was a definite turn-on
the idea of his eagerness excited her
mentally, she caressed his qualities
a tiny glow cheered her
she tried to assess his unreadable features
she felt wrapped in an invisible warmth
her emotions melted her resolve
his invitation was a passionate challenge, hard to resist
she wasn't sure she liked the suggestive tone of his voice

despite his closed expression, she sensed his vulnerability

everything took on a clean brightness when he was around

her feelings for him were intensifying

he struck a vibrant chord in her

she was entranced by the silent sadness of his face

he brought her untried senses to life

she longed for the protectiveness of his arms

aching for the fulfillment of his lovemaking

his nearness made her senses spin

it was too easy to get lost in the way he looked at her

she was caught up in his enthusiasm

she felt a certain sadncss that their day was ending

it wrapped around her like a warm blanket

she felt a curious swooping pull at her innards

she was totally entranced by his compelling personage

she felt like a breathless girl of eighteen

she couldn't deny the spark of excitement at the prospect

she was entirely caught up in her own emotions

her feelings for him had nothing to do with reason

she found herself studying his profile

she studied the lean dark-skinned face

she deliberately shut out any awareness of him

she pulled away, fighting back the tears

she refused his smug gesture of help

her breathing began to settle down to a more even beat

for a long moment she felt as if she were floating

she felt the movement of his breathing

her body felt heavy and warm

her pulse skittered alarmingly

the noise drowned out the thudding of her heart

a delicious shudder heated her body

the glimpses of his strong gold body made her heart beat more rapidly

she looked up and her heart lurched madly

she was shocked at the impact of his gentle grip

he was so very good-looking and she reacted so strongly to him

he was so compelling, his magnetism was so potent

his compelling eyes riveted her to the spot

her heart hammering in her ears

her heartbeat throbbed in her ears

he was so handsome in his black tux that her breath caught in her throat

she couldn't tear her gaze from his profile

her heart fluttered wildly in her breast

she could feel his heart thudding against her own

his vitality still captivated her

there was some tangible bond between them

she froze as her senses leapt to life

it was a purely sensual experience

she was quickly infected by his enthusiasm

she felt her pulses suddenly leap with excitement

he stood so close she could feel the heat from his body

she wanted him to find her desirable

it made her feel good, she was glad to be with him

aware of the strength and warmth of his flesh

in her haste to reassure him, she went too far

her reaction was swift and violent

her instinctive response to him was so powerful

she thought she detected a flicker in his intense eyes

he projected an energy and power that undeniably attracted her

his nearness was overwhelming

she cleared her throat, pretending not to be affected

her heart pounded an erratic rhythm

she couldn't help but notice the tingle of excitement inside her

she tingled as he said her name

she swallowed tightly as he dropped down next to her

she felt the electricity of his touch

at the base of her throat a pulse beat and swelled as though her heart had risen from its usual place

she moved toward him, impelled involuntarily by her own passion

a delightful shiver of wanting ran through her

her pulse quickened at the speculation

her heart thumped erratically

his nearness kindled feelings of fire

her knees were weakened by the quivering of her limbs

her heart thudded noisily within her

his hands on her shoulders sent an involuntary chill through her

his touch upset her balance

the sweetly intoxicating musk of his body overwhelmed her

a rush of pink stained her cheeks

their closeness was like a drug, lulling her to euphoria

her heart thudded once, then settled back to its natural rhythm

his look was so galvanizing it sent a tremor through her

a shudder passed through her

she couldn't suppress an exclamation of admiration

her cheeks colored under the heat of his gaze

their eyes locked as their breathing came in unison

he was even more stunningly virile than she remembered

she bit her lip to stifle the outcry of delight

her heart took a perilous leap

she was filled with a strange inner excitement

she gave a genuine exclamation of delight

her heart seemed to rush to the spot he touched

her breast tingled against the silky fabric of her blouse

her heart thumped uncomfortably

a quiver surged through her veins

she heaved an affronted sigh

before she even turned around, she knew he was there

her heart hammered against her ribs

her wildly beating heart was the only sound audible

explosive currents raced through her

the teasing tone excited her despite silent protestations

her fingers ached to reach over and touch him

her heart began to hammer in her chest

she waited until her quickened pulse subsided

the pounding of her heart finally quieted

she couldn't miss the musky smell of him as he pressed her closer

his touch was oddly soft and caressing

she tried to deny the pulsing knot that had formed in her stomach

the caress was a command

a knot rose in her throat

she waited until her quickened pulse had quieted

a passionate fluttering arose at the back of her neck

a hot ache grew in her throat

she implored him with her eyes

the answer was a rapid thud of her pulse

he made no attempt to hide the fact that he was watching her

his mouth throbbed with a passionate message

the nearness of him gave her comfort

she tried to ignore the strange aching in her limbs

she was only marginally aware of his assessment

she felt the blood surge from her fingertips to her toes

with a giddy sense of pleasure she let her happiness show

she felt her pulse beat in her throat

she gasped in delight

pulled by the vitality zinging through her

felt it racing through her bloodstream

her heartbeat skyrocketed

she felt blood coursing through her veins like an awakened river

she made a quick involuntary appraisal of his features

she inhaled sharply at the contact

her flesh prickled at his touch

she felt an immediate and total attraction

the harsh uneven rhythm of her breathing

a familiar shiver of awareness

a brief shiver rippled through her

she was enjoying his closeness as he checked his long stride to match her own

her heart was hammering foolishly

the pit of her stomach churned

his broad shoulders were heaving as he breathed

his closeness was so male, so bracing

sending shivers of delight through her

she asked playfully, glancing at him

her heart was thundering

she felt drugged by his clean and manly scent

she considered him for a moment, then shrugged

pursing her lips, she thought about him

she hesitated a moment, watching him in profile

her communication skills seemed to have improved

her mind told her to resist, but her body refused

her skin prickled pleasurably

he appraised her with more than mild interest

he talked only to her, ignoring the others

the shock of him ran through her body

they shared an intense physical awareness of each other

an invisible web of attraction building between them

something pulled her attention to him

her heart beat with the pulse of the music

an undeniable magnetism was building between them

she did not want to tear her attention away from him

she wrenched herself away from her ridiculous preoccupation with his arresting face

Touching, Embracing

his large hand took her face and held it gently

he swung her into the circle of his arms

he pulled her roughly, almost violently, to him

twisting in his arms and arching her body, she sought to get free

he swept her, weightless, into his arms

gathering her into his arms, he held her snugly

gently he rocked her back and forth

without looking away, she backed out of his grasp

she buried her face against the corded muscles of his chest

his arms encircled her, one hand in the small of her back

his hands locked against her spine

his hands slipped up her arms, bringing her closer

he whispered into her hair

the touch of his hand was suddenly almost unbearable in its tenderness

she buried her face against his throat

as his grip tightened his attitude became more serious

she put her arms around his neck

in one forward motion, she was in his arms

suddenly she was lifted into the cradle of his arms

he stepped forward and clasped her body tightly to his

her soft curves molding to the contours of his lean body

she could feel his uneven breathing on her cheek, as he held her close

he wrapped his arms around her midriff

as though his words released her, she flung herself against him

his hands explored the hollows of her back

putting a large hand to her waist, he drew her form to him

he whispered, his breath hot against her ear

her eyelashes fluttered against his cheek

the warmth of his arms was so male, so bracing

she locked herself into his embrace

burying her hands in his thick hair

the magnificent man in her arms

at last, reluctantly, they parted a few inches

her head fit perfectly in the hollow between his shoulder and neck

she relaxed, sinking into his cushioning embrace

his embrace encompassed more than her waist

she dropped her chin on his chest with a sigh of pleasure

her trembling limbs clung to him

she had no desire to back out of his embrace

she settled back, enjoying the feel of his arms around her

his touch, firm and persuasive, invited more

she wound her arms inside his jacket and around his back

his breath was warm and moist against her face, and her heart raced

the mere touch of his hand sent a warming shiver through her

she was conscious of where his warm flesh touched her

her skin tingled when he touched her

the occasional jolt of his thigh brushing her hip

her body tingled from the contact

softly his breath fanned her face

she came up behind him, her arms locking around his waist

Kisses

---

reclaiming her lips, he crushed her to him

her calm was shattered with the hunger of his kisses

his kiss was slow, thoughtful

his tongue sent shivers of desire racing through her

his tongue traced the soft fullness of her lips

his tongue explored the recesses of her mouth

he kissed her with his eyes

her lips were still warm and moist from his kiss

giving herself freely to the passion of his kiss

the kiss sent the pit of her stomach into a wild swirl

the caress of his lips on her mouth and along her body set her aflame

his mouth covered hers hungrily

the strong hardness of his lips

his kiss sent new spirals of ecstasy through her

his lips were hard and searching

the cruel ravishment of his mouth

his kiss was surprisingly gentle

his kiss was punishing and angry

she felt the heady sensation of his lips against her neck

she kissed him with a hunger that belied her outward calm

his lips were more persuasive than she cared to admit

his lips brushed against hers as he spoke

raising his mouth from hers, he gazed into her eyes

he kissed the pulsing hollow at the base of her throat

his moist, firm mouth demanded a response

he brushed a gentle kiss across her forehead

his lips pressed against hers, then gently covered her mouth

leaving her mouth burning with fire

he moved his mouth over hers, devouring its softness

his last words were smothered on her lips

burying her face in his neck, she breathed a kiss there

his kiss sang through her veins

standing on tiptoe, she touched her lips to his

his slow, drugging kisses

even in remembrance, she felt the intimacy of his kisses

his kiss was urgent and exploratory

she was shocked at her own eager response to the touch of his lips

her mind relived the velvet warmth of his kiss

his lips continued to explore her soft ivory flesh

the touch of his lips was a delicious sensation

parting her lips, she raised herself to meet his kiss

his demanding lips caressed hers

his lips left hers to nibble at her earlobe

his lips seared a path down her neck, her shoulders

his lips recaptured hers, more demanding this time

she felt his lips touch her like a whisper

she returned his kiss with reckless abandon

she was forced to endure his punishing kiss

he kissed the tip of her nose

the touch of his lips on hers sent a shock wave through her entire body

his lips feather-touched her with tantalizing persuasion

she had a burning desire, an aching need, for another kiss

her lips burned in the aftermath of his fiery possession

he pressed her lips to his, caressing her mouth more than kissing it

the kiss was like the soldering heat that joins metals

he pressed a kiss in her palm before replying

his vow was sealed with a kiss

he smothered her lips with demanding mastery

he took her mouth with a savage intensity

it was divine ecstasy when he kissed her

his mouth did not become softer as he kissed her

she kissed his chin

crushing her to him, he pressed his mouth to hers

his lips slowly descended to meet hers

she quivered at the sweet tenderness of his kiss

he showered kisses around her lips and along her jaw

his mouth swooped down to capture hers

between each word, he planted kisses on her shoulders, neck, and face

his lips came coaxingly down on hers

she drank in the sweetness of his kiss

a kiss as tender and light as a summer breeze

forcing her lips open with his thrusting tongue

he planted a tantalizing kiss in the hollow of her neck

she kissed him, lingering, savoring every moment

her lips found their way instinctively to his

his kiss was as challenging as it was rewarding

kissing her devouringly

she drew his face to hers in a renewed embrace

his lips parted hers in a soul-reaching massage

she succumbed to the forceful domination of his lips

his mouth grazed her earlobe

their lips met and she felt buffeted by the winds of a savage harmony

he kissed the top of her head

near-kisses wouldn't cause her to swoon

she pressed her open lips to his

his lips were warm and sweet on hers

there was a dreamy intimacy to their kiss now

she felt her knees weaken as his mouth descended

a series of slow, shivery kisses

she felt his lips brush her brow

the kiss left her weak and confused

first he kissed the tip of her nose, then her eyes, and, finally, he satisfyingly kissed her soft mouth

it was a kiss for her tired soul to melt into

leaving her mouth burning with fire

she was shocked at her own eager response to the touch of his lips

the gentle massage sent currents of desire through her

shivers of delight followed his touch

as he roused her passion, his own grew stronger

her consciousness seemed to ebb and then flame more distinct than ever

she felt transported on a soft and wispy cloud

her thoughts spun

her emotions whirled and skidded

pleasure radiated outward

her senses reeled as if short-circuited

she breathed lightly between parted lips

blood pounded in her brain, leapt from her heart, and made her knees tremble

Lovemaking

gently he eased her down onto the bed

his lips touched her nipple with tantalizing possessiveness

he fondled one small globe, its pink nipple marble hard

his hand unbuttoned her blouse, his fingers icy, but the palm fiery hot

his tongue caressed her sensitive swollen nipples

his hands slid across her silken belly

gently his hand outlined the circle of her breast

her breasts surged at the intimacy of his touch

he traced his fingertip across her lip

his tongue tantalized the buds which had swollen to their fullest

he eased the lacy cup of her bra aside

his hand moved under her dress to skim her hips and thighs

her dress crept up onto her thighs as she moved closer to him

his hand seared a path down her abdomen and onto her thigh

the gentle massage sent currents of desire through her

his touch was light and painfully teasing

his heartbeat throbbed against her ear

exploring her thighs and then moving up

his lips teased a taut dusky pink nipple

his tongue made a path down her ribs to her stomach

his hands searched for pleasure points

one hand slid down her taut stomach to the swell of her hips

she curled into the curve of his body

the sleek caress of his body

his ardor was surprisingly, touchingly, restrained

he paused to kiss her, whispering his love for each part of her body

his hands moved gently down the length of her back

the stroking of his fingers sent pleasant jolts through her

his hands caressed the planes of her back

she matched his urgency with her own lusty, unsated needs

his hands moved magically over her smooth breasts

he took her hands, encouraging them to explore

she was gathered against a warm pulsing body

he began to slip his hands up her arms, ever so slowly

unbuttoning her blouse with trembling fingers

he gave her a quivering, tentative touch

she caressed the length of his back

instinctively, her body arched toward him

he was running his thumb deliciously up and down her palm

his hands explored the soft lines of her back, her waist, her hips

she caressed the strong tendons in the back of his neck

aroused now, she drew herself closer to him

his hands lightly traced a path over her skin

his hands slipped inside the neckline of her blouse

he rubbed the bare skin of her back and shoulders

his hands explored the soft lines of her waist, her hips

his lips traced a sensuous path to ecstasy

she moaned softly as he lay her down

his tongue explored the rosy peaks of her breasts

her nipples firmed instantly under his touch

his body moved to partially cover hers

his hands began a lust-arousing exploration of her soft flesh

bodily he lifted her and laid her on the bed

his body imprisoned hers in a web of growing arousal

his hands roamed intimately over her breasts

the cool brush of his fingers on her skin

the rosy peaks grew to pebble hardness

he undressed her slowly, worshipfully

she gasped as he lowered his body over hers

it was flesh against flesh, man against woman

her breasts tingled against his hair-roughened chest

she writhed beneath him, eager to touch his skin

his lips brushed her nipples

her nipples, taut beneath the thin fabric

his tormented groan was a heady invitation

she lay panting, her chest heaving

they were able to take the time to explore, to arouse, to give each other pleasure

her body squirmed beneath him

his hard body was atop hers

his hands lifted her robe above her hips

tucking her curves neatly into his own contours

the shapely beauty of her naked body taunted him

quickly she slid out from beneath him

his hand lightly touched her hardening nipples

their bodies naked and still moist from their lovemaking

she didn't protest when his hands sought the buttons of her blouse

he slid the gown off her shoulders, down her arms

discarding her clothes, she stood naked beneath his gaze

bringing their pink tips to crested peaks

she gasped as bare chest met bare chest

taking her hand, he guided it to himself

her full young breasts budded with pink

the light rippled on her ivory breasts

she lay in the haven of his love

outlining the tips of her breasts with his fingers

she felt her breasts crush against the hardness of his chest

skin to skin, they were as one

he kissed her taut nipples, rousing a melting sweetness within her

slowly his hands moved downward, skimming either side of her body to her thighs

he explored her thighs then moved up to her taut stomach

she snuggled against him as their legs intertwined

his hand caressed the skin of her thigh

she trailed tickling fingers up and down his back

his fingers burned into her tingling skin

he picked up a lock of her hair and caressed it gently

passion pounded the blood through her heart, chest, and head

her body felt as if it was half ice and half flame

she breathed in deep soul-drenching drafts

her impatience grew to explosive proportions

his expert touch sent her to even higher levels of ecstasy

love flowed in her like warm honey

she shattered into a million glowing stars

she cried out for release

together they found the tempo that bound their bodies together

their bodies were in exquisite harmony with one another

soaring higher until the peak of delight was reached

exploding in a downpour of fiery sensations

contentment and peace flowed between them

she lay drowned in a floodtide of the liberation of her mind and body

waves of ecstasy throbbed through her

succumbing to the numbed sleep of the satisfied lover

she welcomed him into her body

her body melted against his and the world was filled with him

the pleasure was pure and explosive

she desperately needed more of him than that first touch

the real world spun and careened on its axis

she gasped in sweet agony

she fantasized an even deeper ecstasy

while he would be merely filling a moment of physical desire, she would be allowing him to tear apart her soul

she felt her defenses weakening

the involuntary tremors of arousal began

the feeling was much more than sexual desire

shattering the hard shell that she had built so carefully

a golden wave of passion and love flowed between them

the feel of his rough skin against hers exalted her

the fire spread to her heart

her senses were spun by the scent of his freshly showered body

the warmth of his soft flesh was intoxicating

his hands rested casually on her shoulders, causing her flesh to tingle

she sensed his thrill of arousal

the degree to which she responded stunned her

an electric shock had scorched through her body

his touch was divine ecstasy

she rose to meet him in a moment of uncontrolled passion

a deep feeling of peace entered her being

his raw sensuousness carried her to greater heights

a bright flare of desire sprang into her eyes

she was fully aware of the hardness of his thigh brushing against hers

her eager response matched his

the concave hollow of her spine tingled at his touch

she was too emotion-filled to speak

she responded to the seduction of his passion

a spurt of hungry desire spiraled through her

her love consumed her in desire

her skin prickled with the heat of his touch

her body ached for his touch

her desire for him overrode everything else

his touch sent tingles up her arm

her body still craved his hands

she was filled with an amazing sense of completeness

heat rippled under her skin as she recognized the flush of sexual desire she hadn't felt for months

the dormant sexuality of her body had been awakened

she couldn't disguise her body's reaction

her heart bursting with love and anguish

her breath came in long, surrendering moans

she could feel the heat of his body course down the entire length of hers

shivers of delight followed his touch

as he roused her passion, his own grew stronger

she couldn't control the outcry of delight

she moaned aloud with an erotic pleasure

she knew that the moment of ecstasy had passed

she yielded to the searing need which had been building for months

a moan of ecstasy slipped through her lips

his hardness electrified her

her whole being flooded with desire

passion inched through her veins

she was roused to the peak of desire

he sensed the awakening flames within her

sighed in pleasant exhaustion

she felt an awakened response deep within her

she was hurtled beyond the point of return

the flames of passion burned within both of them

she was dismayed at the magnitude of her own desire

the passion of his ardor mounted

she never dreamed his hands would feel so warm, so gentle

hypnotized by his touch, she tingled under his fingertips

sweetly draining all her doubts and fears

she was drawn to a height of passion she had never known before

she surrendered completely to his masterful seduction

she exalted at the male strength, the cleanliness and beauty of him

passion radiated from the soft core of her body

she wanted to yield to the burning sweetness that seemed captive within her

her body began to vibrate with liquid fire

a tremor inside her heated her thighs and groin

soared to an awesome, shuddering ecstasy

she felt the hysteria of delight rising inside her

she knew the flooding of uncontrollable joy

he freed in her a bursting of sensations

gusts of desire shook her

her lips quivered in unspoken passion

she felt passion rising in her like the hottest fire, clouding her brain

an ache was sparked by that one indelible kiss

she was a glowing image of fire, passion, and love

she abandoned herself to the whirl of sensation

electricity seemed to arc through her

her thoughts fragmented as his hands and lips continued their hungry search of her body

the turbulence of his passion swirled around her

the hot tide of passion raged through both of them

it was a raw act of possession

she savored the feeling of satisfaction he left with her

Miscellaneous

Fatigue

she shivered with chill and fatigue

fatigue settled in pockets under her eyes

she was so tired her nerves throbbed

she lost weight and appeared tired and haggard

she felt achy and exhausted

her face was pale and pinched

she pressed both hands over her eyes as if they burned with weariness

her eyes burned dryly from sleeplessness

she aroused herself from the numbness that weighed her down

she was finally exhausted and sensually disturbed

drifting back into wisps of sleep

her whole body was engulfed in tides of weariness and despair

she sighed, weary of the argument

she felt drained, hollow, lifeless

she felt as hollow as her voice sounded

shadows deepened under her eyes

weariness enveloped her as she tried to concentrate

with a long, exhausted sigh, he stood up

she had felt listless all day

her exhausted eyes smiled at him

as the tepid water washed away her tiredness

her eyes were ringed with black circles

her muscles screamed from the strain

she felt empty and drained

she wondered at the cause of her weariness

her back ached between her shoulder blades

his usually lively eyes sparkled with weariness

Memories

---

her memories of him were pure and clear

her mind burned with the memory

he mused on some private memories, his face sober

his name lingered around the edges of her mind

she lay down, but her mind returned to its tortured thinking

as the image focused in her memory, she could see again

their names kept slipping through her thoughts

she remembered the aftermath

with a shiver of vivid recollection

she suffered the dull ache of desire at the thought of him

she consoled herself with the reminder

her mind kept turning to last night

she would never forget a single detail of his face

she hungered from the memory of his mouth on hers

his name echoed in the black stillness of her mind

she could still feel the warm grip of his handshake

for some time after he had gone, she felt a warm glow

she recalled the ecstasy of being held against his strong body

in spite of her busy schedule, thoughts of him intruded into her day

her thoughts filtered back to the day she'd met him

her own words returned to haunt her the following day

she clung to that memory as she would to a life preserver in a stormy sea

her face burned as she remembered

she remembered the keen probing eyes and inscrutable expression

the eyes in the gaunt face came back to her

her blood soared with unbidden memories

her musings were interrupted by a male voice

she was trapped by the memory of her own emotions

the memory brought a wry, twisted smile to her face

the memory of the bruising kiss came back

she tried to keep the memory pure and unsullied

he left a burning imprint on her

her lips tingled in remembrance of his touch

another round of painful memories

a cold shiver spread over her as she remembered

subconsciously aware of the dull ache at the memory

recalling the smoldering passion that had thrilled her

his face haunted her, smiling, serious, or thoughtful

she savored the feeling of satisfaction he left with her

his sensuousness threatened to rekindle old forgotten feelings

he was gentle and loving then

Questions, Intrigue, Curiosity

she asked, wanting to put all the pieces together

pensively, she looked out into the darkness

she could not stop herself from pondering

she began to wonder just what she wanted of him

she regarded him with somber curiosity

she wondered if she should feel some guilt for the relief she felt

she wondered if he could be baiting her

ceaseless, inward questions

the suggestion intrigued her

the question hammered at her

ignoring the mocking voice inside that wondered why

when was the last time she'd truly enjoyed herself with a man

she was curious, seeing the change on his face

her head was puzzled by new thoughts

wondering idly what had happened since

asked a little voice inside her head

he looked as if he were weighing the question

how could she penetrate the deliberate blankness of his eyes

must his every movement remind her of his sexual attractiveness

a cynical inner voice cut through her thoughts

she began to wonder if there was anything he couldn't do

she wondered how she compared to his other conquests

was his look of enthrallment mirrored in her own face

could she resist his bundle of restless energy

Thoughts, Realizations, Understanding

she had to fight her own battle of personal restraint

she was unable to give herself completely to any man

she found the thought very satisfying

she could no longer deny herself his touch

the day of reckoning can't be postponed forever

she hurtled back to earth as reality struck

she was astonished at the sense of fulfillment she felt

it was an awakening experience that left her reeling

the admission was dredged from a place beyond logic and reason

it was her own driving need that shocked her

masterful persuasion seemed to be his style

if she had expected a yes or no, she had underestimated him

she knew there was something special about him from the very beginning

her heart swelled with a feeling she had thought long since dead

she thought with fearful clarity

the harder she tried to ignore the truth the more it persisted

the thought froze in her brain

something clicked in her mind

it came as no surprise to see him there

her vow not to become involved shattered

opening her eyes, she came back to reality

she was contrite and shocked at the depth of his feelings

all too quickly she ran out of diversions

the undeniable and dreadful facts

he gave her too much of everything but himself

the thought barely crossed her mind before another followed

an even more terrifying realization washed over her

she had known of the strong passion within her

she had begun to recognize her own needs

there was no room for romance in her busy schedule

she needed to be alone with her thoughts

they had reached the point where their relationship had to be resolved she admitted the truth graciously and hopefully

she couldn't deny the evidence any longer

she could sense the barely controlled power that was coiled in his body

it seemed that they disagreed on the very nature and meaning of love

she hadn't realized what a powerful opponent she had chosen

she became instantly awake, fully aware of her surroundings

she couldn't deny the evidence any longer

she impatiently pulled her drifting thoughts together

when he left, she felt an extraordinary void

on safer ground now, she paused to reflect a moment

quickly, she banished the thought

there'd be time for such thoughts later

he seemed pensive, not disturbed or angry

she tucked the thought away

she allowed her subconscious thoughts to surface

looking back, she knew he was kinder than he wanted anyone to know

she lay in the drowsy warmth of her bed, thinking

she was momentarily lost in her own reveries

she was surprised to hear his words echo her own thoughts

her last waking thought before she drifted into sleep

startled by the thought that flashed through her mind

her mind was filled with sour thoughts

Colors

Black

onyx
blue-black
ink
coal
jet
ebony
obsidian
raven
anthracite
black pearl
midnight
shadow
pitch
sable

Purple

amethyst
indigo
violet
lavender
magenta
heliotrope
mauve
plum
wood violet
lilac
orchid

Green

jade
emerald
malachite
kelly
leaf
moss
celadon
sea
hunter
lime
forest
olive
bluish-green
aqua
aquamarine
grass
pea
mist
chartreuse
verdant

White/Off-white

milk
milky quartz
white jade
moonstone
ivory
cream
alabaster
opal
magnolia
vanilla
chalk
oyster
oatmeal
eggshell
ecru
parchment
snow
lily

Gray

smoke
pearl
charcoal
silvery
dove
gunmetal
sooty
tattletale
hoary

Blue

azure
periwinkle
wedgewood
delft
neon
electric
cornflower
turquoise
royal
powder
cobalt
teal
navy
sky
robin's egg
baby
lapis lazuli
indigo
steel
sapphire
federal
marine
ultra marine

Red/Pink

ruby
scarlet
garnet
red amber
rose
dusky rose
rust
crimson
cinnabar
wine
claret
cerise
shrimp
russet
burgundy
ox-blood
carmine
apple
cherry
tomato
brick
terra cotta
brass
ashes of roses
cardinal
Tyrian
rubescent
rubicund
vermillion
vermeil
cochineal
maroon
auburn
strawberry
raspberry
blood
candy apple
beet
currant
Titian
lobster
salmon
fire-engine
coral

Brown/Beige

earth
nutmeg
cinnamon
rust
chocolate
cocoa
dun
tan
chestnut
bay
tawny
roan
mahogany
pecan
rosewood
maple
taupe
coffee
toffee
café au lait
mocha
tortoise shell
brick
ginger
hazel
walnut
henna
brunette
ecru
mushroom
fawn
buckskin
nut brown
umber
saddle
raisin
khaki
drab
bronze
copper
tanned
foxy

Yellow/Gold

fool's gold
blonde
ash blonde
white-gold
platinum
burnished
brass
palomino
honey
silver blonde
primrose
daffodil
jonquil
cadmium
tawny
buff
flaxen
sandy
straw